SOMETHING'S *not* ЯIGHT

One family's struggle with learning disabilities

An autobiography by

NANCY LELEWER

VanderWyk & Burnham
A DIVISION OF PUBLICOM, INC.
Acton, Massachusetts

Dedication

To my mom and dad, who taught me about parenting through their examples of consistency, structure, nurturing, and love and have always found time to listen.

To my four children, who expanded my knowledge of learning and loving and allowed this invasion of their privacy in the hope it would help others.

This publication is sold with the understanding that the publisher is not engaged in rendering legal, psychiatric, or other professional services. If expert assistance is required, the services of a competent professional person should be sought.

Published by VanderWyk & Burnham
A Division of Publicom, Inc.
Acton, Massachusetts

Cover and interior design: Margaret Ong Tsao

Library of Congress Catalog Card Number: 94-60521

Publisher's Cataloging-in-Publication Data

Lelewer, Nancy
Something's Not Right: One family's struggle with learning dis-
    abilities / Nancy Lelewer
Includes resources section.
1. Learning disabled children—Education—United States I. Title
2. Parent and child
LC4705.L   649.152   94-60521

ISBN 0-9641089-0-9 hardcover
ISBN 0-9641089-1-7 paperback

FIRST PRINTING
Manufactured in the United States of America
10 9 8 7 6 5 4 3 2 1

Acknowledgments

Of the many people I want to thank for their help along the way, Lucie Prinz is first on my list. Lucie has read and critiqued every rewrite, and when I despaired about the project, her encouragement helped me get back on track.

For her enthusiasm and expertise in guiding this project through its final stages, I thank my publisher at VanderWyk & Burnham, Meredith Rutter. She and I both express our appreciation to the editor, Patricia Carda, for smoothing the manuscript's rough edges with skill, insight, and sensitivity.

I am also grateful to the following people for their help and support with this book: Dr. Rosemary F. Bowler, Hazel Cherney, John Cox, William H. Davidow, John Davis, Mae B. Davis, Jody Dow, Dr. Charles R. Drake, Andrea Dubroff, Dr. Frank Hopkins Duffy, Wendy Erickson, Diane Frohling, Dr. Albert Galaburda, Mary Hadley, Robert G. Hall, Dr. Howard T. Hermann, Bjorg Jakob-Marum, Miriam Knapp, Dr. E. M. Christine Kris, Joseph Lelewer, Sis Lelewer, Stanley Lelewer, Dr. Gary Marple, David Maxon, Dr. David McAnulty, Dr. Gloria McAnulty, Maggie Miller, Robert Nazzarro, Carolyn Oliver, Pamela Painter, Sally Powers, Margaret Byrd Rawson, Ken Rivard, Dr. Laura Lehtinen Rogan, Kathy Rowe, Nancy Schmidt, Dr. Larry B. Silver, Bob Sinclair, Valery Sinclair, Ben Slomoff, Sylvia Slomoff, Eric Sonnabend, Alan Trustman, Dr. Per Udden, Barbie Ullman, Sandy Ullman, Lelene Volk, and Patti Wagner.

Contents

Preface

I grew up in a house where reading was not a major activity. My parents read parts of the newspaper daily, some magazine articles and books occasionally, but no one in my family ever sat for hours reading.

My mother, a college graduate, has always been plagued with letter reversals, number inversions, and speaking in mala-props (misusing words) or rephrasings. "The Voice of the Turtle" comes out "The Turtle Speaks."

My father, a successful businessman and exceptional athlete, was a low-average student. In elementary school and high school, he was more interested in playing sports than in studying, and after two years of college he dropped out to go into business. Even so, he still vividly remembers an experience that happened eighty-one years ago, when he was seven: "The headmaster came into our first-grade classroom and asked each youngster to spell a word. When I spelled *away* 'a-y-a-w,' he said, 'You flunk and will have to repeat high first.' My teacher told the headmaster that I was a bright and conscientious child and convinced him I should be promoted to low second."

Over the years, professionals from various disciplines have used many names in their efforts to find a good identifying term for the frustrating problem of a child's failure to learn even in a good educational environment and even with good motivation (until defeat has begun to erode it). Among the names professionals have tried are minimal brain damage, perceptual handicap, learning disabilities, dyslexia, and more recently, learning differences. All refer to a syndrome that is made up of complicated sets of varying conditions that manifest themselves in myriad ways.

Dyslexia is one form of learning disability that has its own name. It is distinguished, in part, by its own patterns of strong and weak abilities that may differ from patterns in other learning disabilities. Dyslexia is a syndrome that, stated most simply, inhibits one's ability to read or to use language. It is never as simple as confusing "b" for "d" or "was" for "saw," although that is often part of the problem. It has nothing to do with one's inherent intelligence—some biographers have suggested that Einstein was dyslexic.

Although neither of my parents was ever diagnosed as dyslexic (the syndrome was hardly recognized when they were growing up), I suspect they both have mild learning disabilities. Dyslexia runs in my family. I have a bright and creative first cousin who was tutored around the clock and who had to change schools frequently for academic and behavior reasons. I myself am dyslexic, as are three of my four children, their father, and at least one of my children's first cousins.

My children actually display a range of learning disabilities, from severe to none. Whitney, my second daughter, has no learning disability at all. As you will read, Brian, my son, had and has many problems in addition to dyslexia, including visual/motor/perceptual disabilities, "language unscrambling" problems, and hyperactivity. His story forms the majority of this book because his problems showed up very early and required the most attention. Hyperactivity was present in two of my four children. With today's focus on ADD (Attention Deficit Disorder), not necessarily a learning disability in itself, although the two are frequently found together, I believe that this label also may be applied to all three of my learning-disabled children.

Over the years I have received hundreds of phone calls from desperate families. I have listened to their stories, made suggestions and referrals, and emphasized that one person, usually the mother, has to take the responsibility for finding and coordinating all necessary people and resources that will enable their learning-disabled child to learn. With all the literature, special schools, and tutors available today, it is shocking to find the number of children, teenagers, and young adults who are still not receiving the appropriate education.

Frequently, the parents I speak to have learned or come to suspect their child has a learning disability because the child is doing poorly academically and may have started acting out or may have been caught cheating. Unfortunately, many of these parents don't know exactly what their child's strengths and weaknesses are, nor do they know how their child learns. Answers to these questions, whether gleaned through parental observation or direct testing by trained personnel, are essential if an appropriate educational program is to be developed and implemented. Without a tailored program, the child's chances of success both in school and in life are greatly reduced.

Most LD children have average or above average intelligence. Most do not have the severity of learning problems my son had. Like my two LD daughters and myself, most have quite normal preschool years; the disabilities remain hidden until the child is unable to cope with one or more academic requirements. Once learning disabilities do surface, they interfere with many (in some cases, all) aspects of the person's life until the individual learns to compensate for them.

If you are a parent of a child with a learning disability, I want to impress on you the necessity of early diagnosis and remediation. I want to stress the importance of your role as a parent. And I want to give you hope. LD children can learn to learn. They can become normal, happy, productive adults. It is the responsibility of parents to give their children this chance.

I've written this book about our family to bring a better awareness and understanding of learning disabilities to the general public. I am very grateful to my children for allowing this invasion of their privacy. Although every event is described as it happened, I have chosen to publish under my maiden name and to change many other names in the book in order to protect others' privacy. Therefore, if you try to locate certain people named in my story, you may be frustrated. If, after reading this book, you want more information because the phrase "something's not right" describes a child you know, please contact the organizations and read the materials listed in the Representative Resources section at the back of this book. You will be on the right path.

A Poem on Learning Disabilities

The college dean says:
"Such rawness in a student is a shame—
'Tis lack of preparation is to blame!"

The high school principal says:
"Good heavens, what crudity! The boy's a fool!
The fault of course is in the elementary school."

The elementary school principal says:
"Would that from such a dunce I might be spared.
They send them up to me so unprepared."

The primary principal says:
"Poor kindergarten blockhead! And they call that preparation?
Worse than none at all!"

The kindergartner says:
"Such lack of training did I never see—
What sort of a person can the mother be!"

The mother says:
"You stupid child! But then you're not to blame.
Your father's family are all the same."

—ANNA GILLINGHAM

From *The First Seven Years of The Gillingham Reading Program at the Francis W. Parker School,* 1957. Reprinted by permission of Robert G. Hall, Educators Publishing Service.

Introduction

My First Reading Test

"I stared at the page and total panic gripped me."

—Nancy

My children were born in the late 1950s and early 1960s, when little was known about hyperactivity or learning disabilities. Such syndromes then confounded the experts, who only spoke in terms of "exceptional" children—those who were emotionally disturbed or mentally retarded. Most experts thought learning disabilities could be handled by traditional tutoring. Hyperactivity bewildered them.

Even today, more than thirty years later, I get angry when I look back and remember those experts' comments and how my children had to fight to learn. But when I look back, I also remember my first introduction to dyslexia.

I began public elementary school in the early 1940s in Highland Park, Illinois, a suburb on the north shore of Chicago, which was known for its educational excellence. Reading was taught exclusively by a whole-word method dubbed "Look, Say" because of its reliance on recognizing

15

individual words as whole visual patterns, rather than focusing on letters or letter patterns. In first grade, I listened to my classmates, and when it was my turn, I read the pictures, not the words, "Oh Sally! See Spot. Run. Run. Run." When we were shown flash cards and responded in unison to them, I mouthed something.

Then came our first reading test. The teacher handed each student a sheet of paper, the top half of which was covered with writing. I looked at it and couldn't read a word. The bottom half of the page had a vertical column of boxes down the left side. To the right of each box was a string of words that I also couldn't read. The teacher said to read the paragraph at the top of the sheet and then read the sentences underneath it. We were to mark a "T" in each box preceding a sentence that was true and an "F" in each box preceding a sentence that was false. The room grew quiet as the class began to read.

As I stared at the page, total panic gripped me. My insides churned, and I began to perspire as I wondered what I was going to do. As it happened, the boy who sat right in front of me was the most able reader in my class. Within a few minutes, he had completed the test and had pushed his paper to the front of his desk, which put it in my full view. I saw that he had filled the boxes on his paper with T, F, F, T, F, and I proceeded to put the same letters in the boxes on my paper. What luck! I passed the test and was off on a track of living by my wits rather than being able to read.

The "wits track" is a nerve-wracking one. I worried that the boy would be out sick on the day we had a reading test. I worried that the teacher might change the location of my desk. I worried that I would get caught copying another student's answers. I knew that something was wrong with me, but I didn't know what. Why couldn't I recognize words that my classmates read so easily? Because everyone praised me when I did well on tests, I did my best to hide my inadequate reading skills.

First grade was difficult, but by the end of the year I was able to read a few words. Fortunately, I was at the top of my math class. Unfortunately, students were not allowed to count on their fingers, and that was the only way I could do the calculations. So, I hid my hands in my pockets. Mother wanted me in dresses and skirts, but somehow I managed to sidestep her and wear trousers or my cousin's old knickers. My mother assumed that I liked wearing pants because I enjoyed climbing trees and playing football, which was true, but the real reason was that I needed the pockets in which to hide my fingers while I did my computations. Although my reading and spelling were appalling, my prowess in math, after its fashion, reassured me that I wasn't totally stupid.

Another saving grace was that I was a good athlete. I was always the first or second person chosen for a team, which added to my self-confidence and made me a member of "the gang." This was in reassuring contrast to the precocious boy who sat in front of me in reading. He could neither run fast nor hit a ball. He was usually one of the last chosen for a team and was treated as an outsider by the popular kids.

Although my start in school was inauspicious, I was fortunate to have several extremely outstanding teachers as the years went on. With their patience and help and my extra effort, I managed to complete elementary school and then high school with A's and B's.

Actually, one of the B's was a gift. Biology, my sophomore year in high school, was impossible. I simply couldn't retain everything I was memorizing, including all the plant and animal phyla. Even those I remembered, I misspelled. I did my best, but by the end of the year, it was all a big jumble in my head. Mr. McMullen, my teacher, called my father after the final exam and said, "I just burned Nancy's biology exam and am giving her a B for the year." He went on to explain that I was very bright, had done all the homework correctly and on time, listened well in class, and would need the B to get into a good college, which was where I belonged. "Her exam was the worst I've seen," he added. "Don't let her take any more science courses."

As I watched my children grow, I couldn't escape the notion that they were in some way extensions of myself, and if something was wrong with them, it was because something was wrong with me. Although that thought tormented me, it gave me a subtle strength because I knew, notwithstanding my handicap, through hard work and determination I had always managed to succeed. Surely, then, my children would. So I struggled on, trying to find answers, trying not to think negatively, and trying to focus my energies on the business at hand. In my son's case, the business at hand was a slow, step-by-step process of elimination calculated to identify pathways to his painfully isolated intelligence.

Over the years I kept in touch with Mr. McMullen, my biology teacher. Years later, after the children were grown and I had begun my dyslexia research at the Massachusetts Institute of Technology, I called Mac and said, "I thought you'd like to know that I just got an appointment to the man/vehicle lab in the Department of Aeronautics and Astronautics at MIT." He laughed and said, "Oh, my, now this country is really in trouble."

1

Brian's Introduction into the World

"The baby is shaking. His whole body is trembling."

—Nurse at Beth Israel Hospital

In response to the essay question on my Sarah Lawrence College application, "Who is the woman you most admire?" I had written about Eleanor Roosevelt. Now, seated between my parents and Jay, my husband to be, I listened to the former First Lady give our commencement speech.

I had struggled for four years to get through the long reading and writing assignments. I had studied days, nights, and many weekends, and I was proud and relieved I'd successfully completed my formal education. The sun was warm on that perfect spring day in 1957, and I looked forward to what was then assumed to be life's next stage—marriage and children.

That September Jay and I were married in Chicago, honeymooned in Mexico, and rented a town house in Brookline, Massachusetts, the Boston suburb where my husband had grown up. I felt fortunate to have fallen in love with and married a man who was not only wonderful but also a man of some means, and I was sure that life would be good now that the difficult school days were behind me. The future looked very promising.

Nine months later, Kelly, our first child, arrived. Whitney, our second, arrived sixteen months after Kelly. Even allowing for parental pride, they were beautiful and lovable babies. Both girls seemed to do everything according to Dr. Spock. At the age when babies are supposed to be able to sit unsupported, they sat unsupported. They walked when they were supposed to walk. They talked when they were supposed to talk. In fact, it sometimes seemed that Kelly *never stopped* walking and talking. She flittered around the house touching everything, climbing on the furniture, even scaling shelves, and always telling me about everything she had seen and heard during the day. Whitney was her faithful shadow. They looked so much alike as toddlers that people often thought they were twins.

Wanting more room and our own backyard for the girls to play in, we purchased and moved into a beautiful home a few miles away from where we lived. We knew we wanted to make some alterations, but for the moment, it gave the girls space to run in, which they did.

In June 1961, when Kelly was three years old and Whitney was twenty months, I hired a college girl named Jeannie to help care for them over the summer. I was especially grateful for her help because we had finally decided to go ahead with some major structural alterations. The kitchen was being expanded into a combination breakfast room/kitchen and a family room, and a whole new second floor was being added to give us two more bedrooms and a bath. Workmen wandered in and out of the house on a daily basis as the children ran through the mess that alterations entail.

I hoped to be able to fill one of the new bedrooms with our third child. We thought I had conceived in June, but in July I started to stain, and an early pregnancy test proved negative. I was disappointed, but I was confident I would soon be pregnant.

In August, my husband, the girls, Jeannie, and I vacationed in Rockland, Maine, to escape the workmen, the mess of renovation, and Boston's heat. That was about all I escaped. I was frequently nauseated in the mornings, and by evening, I was surprised that I could feel so tired while on vacation. One day I flew to Boston, just for the day, to oversee the construction and pick up our second car, which had been left in the shop for repairs. That afternoon I nearly fell asleep driving from Brookline back to Rockland.

By the end of August, it was obvious that I was pregnant, and the only question was whether my due date was March or April, because my last real period had been in June. This pregnancy seemed more difficult than the previous two, but I thought things would soon settle down, and I was excited about the prospect of a new baby.

In September we returned to our Brookline house, which was covered with plaster dust and still didn't have a usable kitchen. But we coped, shifting around among the rooms and dealing with its endearing tampered-with-ranch eccentricities. Jeannie was still with us, which was lifesaving.

My husband's company was opening a new branch hotel in the Caribbean at the end of the month, and Jeannie agreed to stay with the girls while we attended the ceremonies. I knew I wouldn't have to worry about the children with Jeannie there. She was wonderful with them. She loved playing with them, and she also did the laundry, fixed meals, and had a knack for getting the girls into bed on time. Jay and I were scheduled to fly to New York and from there continue on to the island paradise. I was tremendously excited about the trip.

A few days before we left, I began to feel sick, but I was so busy with preparations that I ignored the initial symptoms. By the day before our departure, I had a fever and a bad cough that I couldn't ignore any longer. I went to see Dr. Hestor, my internist. After examining me, he gave me a prescription, ordered me to bed, and said if my fever was gone in the morning, I could go on the trip. As I got ready to leave the office, he mentioned taking an X ray, but because I was pregnant, we decided it wasn't a good idea. Instead, he urged me to get plenty of rest while I was on the island.

After two pills and twelve hours' sleep, my temperature was normal. Unfortunately, by the time we reached the hotel in New York City, I was perspiring, and I immediately climbed into bed. In the morning I felt better and we flew on to the Caribbean.

By the time we arrived, my body ached all over, and it hurt when I coughed. Of our stay on the island, I remember only that it was very windy, there was a shortage of cold water in the hotel, and no matter how much cough medicine or how many lozenges I swallowed, I couldn't stop coughing. To add to my misery, Jay kept telling me to stop coughing as it was making a very poor impression. I had an insatiable thirst, the wind on my body felt like a winter gale, and my ribs hurt.

On the fourth day of our trip, I convinced Jay that I needed to return to Boston. When we arrived at Logan Airport, I was too sick to go to our busy home, so Jay took me to a hotel, and I climbed into bed. The next thing I remember was Jay awakening me and telling me that I had slept for two nights and a day. "You've slept enough," he said.

I was disoriented, my chest hurt from coughing, and I was alternately hot and cold. After a shower I felt slightly better and we drove home. The girls came tumbling out to greet us. Hugs and kisses left me so shaky I decided I'd better go to bed. Two bedrooms away I could hear Jeannie packing her clothes to return to school, but I simply couldn't get up. When Jeannie came in to say goodbye, Kelly and Whitney followed her with their stuffed animals and toys so they could play with me on my bed. The remainder of the day is a blur in my memory. That night I truly thought I was going to die, and finally in the early morning hours, I convinced my husband to call Dr. Hestor.

He arrived at 7:30 A.M., awakened me sympathetically, and examined me.

"You have a fever of 106 degrees," he told me. Turning to my husband, he said, "She has viral pneumonia and should be hospitalized. Her condition is contagious."

"She can't go to the hospital," Jay protested. "She has to be here to take care of our children."

"She is in no condition to take care of anyone," Dr. Hestor repeated. "She's contagious—do you understand?—and the children must be kept away from her."

Jay called my mother in Chicago, who said she'd fly to Boston immediately, and Dr. Hestor agreed that I could stay at home only if Jay stayed in the house until my mother arrived. Before Dr. Hestor left, I heard him explain to the girls that their mother needed to rest and that they should play quietly in the playroom.

Caring for me, two toddlers, and our cavernous house wore my mother down very quickly. At almost three and a half, Kelly had a mind of her own, and the word "fear" wasn't in her vocabulary. Kelly liked to run to the top of the stairs, give a leap, stiffen her body, and then zoom down the steps as if she were lying on a slide. Whitney was a little more cautious, and although she often copied Kelly, she never tried this trick. Instead, she would quickly toddle down the stairs after her older sister. Within twenty-four hours of her arrival, Mother hired a woman to help with the children and household chores.

I couldn't move. Drenched with perspiration, I lay shivering in bed. During the days, I could hear Kelly, Whitney, and my mother down the hall talking and giggling, but I was too exhausted to concentrate on what they were saying. When my fever finally broke, I was too weak to walk. To get to the bathroom, I would roll to the other side of the bed, crawl to the bathroom rug, and lie there until I had the energy to pull myself onto the toilet.

As I slowly grew stronger, I began to feel the baby's first signs of life within me—the tiny, reassuring jabs that I'd felt during my other two pregnancies. However, unlike the other times, this time I felt a faint yet constant shaking. Why, I wondered, was this baby shaking? I hadn't felt tremors during my other two pregnancies. I suppressed a wave of foreboding and tried to convince myself all was well.

Visits to my obstetrician in the weeks that followed did little to ease my mind. When I said again and again that I could feel the baby shaking, Dr. Kopans tried to reassure me that the baby was fine. Unable to convince me that I was imagining things, he suggested I talk to a psychiatrist. Instead, I decided to do some research for myself. I went to the library and searched through medical books and journals, but there was nothing on fetuses that shook. Then I thought about babies that shake after birth and read about infants with cerebral palsy, but nothing in that material mentioned pre-birth tremors.

Because people raised their eyebrows, rolled their eyes, and gave me strange looks when I said the baby in me was shaking, I kept busy with my children and friends, and I stopped talking about the tremors, even though they continued. In some way, the tremors I felt within me created a bond between the baby and myself that was even stronger than the bonds I had felt during my first two pregnancies.

We took the girls to Florida for a family reunion with their grandparents at the beginning of March. Two days before our scheduled return, Kelly, with a child's usual sense of perfect timing, came down with chicken pox. Jay had to return to work, but I stayed until Kelly was well enough to travel. Of course, by the time Kelly was healthy, Whitney had the worst case of chicken pox the local pediatrician had ever seen, and the baby, which I had been carrying high, dropped.

My March due date came and went without the appearance of the baby. So, assuming that the baby was not due until April, I gathered up the kids and went home. I was beginning to feel that I had been pregnant for a very long time.

As April drew toward a close without any signs of labor,

Dr. Kopans decided to induce the baby. I entered the hospital early on April 25, 1962. Dr. Kopans put me to sleep, very briefly, to induce labor, but under anesthesia I thrashed around and vomited, making it impossible for him to break the sack. When I awoke, there was some discussion of what to do next. Finally Dr. Kopans told me that if I could hold still without medication, he would try once more to break the sack. At 8:30 A.M. he succeeded. Shortly thereafter, I began having contractions.

A young nurse was assigned to monitor the fetal heartbeat. Every hour or so, she would come in, put her cold stethoscope to my belly, and after listening at several spots, run for a doctor because she couldn't hear a heartbeat. Then a doctor would dash into my room. After encountering a beat, he'd use a pen to mark an X on my belly as a reference point for the nurse. As the hours progressed, so did the X's.

I didn't know why the nurse couldn't find my baby's heartbeat, but her behavior made me very apprehensive. Now I was doubly worried that there was something wrong with the baby.

By 6:00 P.M. I was in heavy labor, but the anesthetist did not administer anesthesia until just before Brian was born. When Brian arrived at 6:30, weighing seven pounds, seven and three-quarters ounces, I was still awake enough to hear the nurse say to me, "You have a beautiful little boy." To Dr. Kopans she said, "The baby is shaking. His whole body is trembling. What do you think is the matter?"

I strained to hear the doctor's reply. "I don't know," he said. "I'm astonished. She said she felt the baby trembling inside her, but I didn't believe her. I've never seen a baby shake like this before." Then the medication took effect.

Early the next morning, I got my first good look at Brian. He was an adorable baby with dark hair and tiny ears pressed flat against the sides of his head. As I held him, I could feel him shake, and the tremors felt just the same as they had when he was in my womb. That reinforced the closeness I had felt toward him when he was inside me. In a sense, he had spoken to me of his need before he was born.

I didn't know then that this sensory communication would be almost our only form of communication for the next several years. Had I known what was ahead of me, I might have despaired. But fortune was kind enough to enlighten me only by degrees.

As it was, the bond that had grown between us before his birth gave me enough insight into Brian that I knew what he could understand and do even when people said he couldn't. To some people, to some professionals, this intuitive connection was a mystery. Often they didn't want to hear my opinion and didn't believe what I said. However, Brian accomplished many things that some people predicted he would never be able to do.

The following day, Dr. Holburn, our pediatrician, examined Brian in the hospital nursery, then came into my room to congratulate me on the birth of my healthy son.

"Why does he shake?" I asked. "What's wrong with him?"

"He may have an underdeveloped nervous system," he said. Then he shrugged and turned up the palms of his hands.

"What does that mean? When will he stop shaking?"

"I don't know," he said. He smiled, patted my shoulder, and left the room.

Was history repeating itself? I wondered apprehensively. My mother had given birth to three children. The first was a son with projectile vomiting. He had lived one year and died of an unknown cause. Then I was born. Before I was two years old, my mother had a second son who was sick from birth, his affliction never diagnosed. He died of pneumonia when he was thirteen months old. My two daughters and I were healthy as horses. Was there something wrong with the male infants in our family?

Five days later we came home from the hospital.

Fortunately, for the first six weeks, I had a marvelous nurse who shared the work with me. It was fortunate because

Brian shook and cried and screamed continuously. He was colicky and often vomited after being nursed, to me a horrifying reminder of my dead brothers.

Sometimes after nursing him, I would burp him, change his diaper, put him on a clean sheet in his crib, and then let him scream. Holding him didn't seem to help, so I tried to outlast him, reasoning that if I didn't pick him up, he would eventually stop crying. But after he had screamed for half an hour or so, I wouldn't be able to bear the screaming any longer, and I'd pick him up again. The only thing that seemed to calm him was motion. Day and night he was walked and rocked. When all else failed, I took him for rides in the car. Sometimes I'd drive fifty or more miles, always hoping to miss the red lights, as he'd wake up and begin to cry if I stopped for more than a few seconds. The days seemed endless. On the nurse's days off, Brian's crying drove me nearly crazy. Although I never imagined doing away with him, a feeling some mothers with colicky babies have confessed to, I began to understand the urge. To keep him quiet on the days without the nurse, I would tuck him under one arm while I cooked, cleaned, played games with the girls, and did whatever else I had to with the other arm. At night, after settling Kelly and Whitney in bed, finishing the dishes, and restoring order to the playroom, I walked and rocked Brian while counting the hours until the nurse's return.

Time and time again, I asked Dr. Holburn why Brian cried so, but he never seemed to have an answer. Since Brian was gaining weight and growing as he should, Dr. Holburn assured me the crying was not important. He did notice that one of Brian's feet turned outward, and so he prescribed a corrective shoe. Every day when I tried to put on the tiny shoe and lace it up, Brian would be kicking and crying so hard that it would be almost impossible to do. Finally I begged the doctor to prescribe something to quiet the crying. He ordered some phenobarbital and suggested I stop nursing. He thought perhaps Brian was allergic to my

27

milk. I thought it was worth trying Brian on the phenobarbital first.

The first time I gave Brian a few drops of phenobarbital shortly before nursing, the results were breathtaking. As the medication took effect, his shaking slowly decreased until it ceased altogether. Instead of seeming frantic, he nursed calmly. As the phenobarbital wore off, the shaking returned, but the milk stayed down and he did not seem as colicky. Before long, his crying decreased to an hour or less per day, but he still kicked and waved his arms incessantly.

Soon he was kicking so much water out of the bathinette that I had to bathe him in the bathtub. At first, this was merely a strain on my back, but one day he clung to me hysterically. The next day he did the same thing. I put on a bathing suit, got into the tub with him, and sat him on my outstretched legs. He hung onto me with a death grip, but I was able to wash him.

Two days after Brian turned six months old, I was bathing him and suddenly realized he was not shaking. I finished washing his hair, dried him, and held him next to me. His body was quiet next to mine. I dressed him and again held him against me. Brian was not shaking. I waited until that night to be sure he didn't start to shake again. My husband was away and couldn't be reached, so I called my parents. "Dad, Brian has stopped shaking!" I exclaimed with tears running down my cheeks.

2

Struggling with Chaos

"How do you do...?"

—Brian

A lthough the first eight months of Brian's life had been a struggle, I still didn't realize the extent of his problems nor the time and energy that would be required to help him. Thus, it didn't worry me when I became pregnant with our fourth child during Brian's first winter. After all, I thought, Brian wasn't crying constantly, and he had stopped shaking. Soon he would be walking and talking, and that would make things even easier. Kelly was a happy-go-lucky four-year-old in her second year of nursery school, and Whitney had just begun her first year of nursery school. It was time for another baby.

On September 29, 1963—when Brian was seventeen months, Whitney was a few days short of her fourth birthday, and Kelly was five years three months old—I went into labor again. It would be the beginning of the most arduous period of my life.

That night I was taken into the delivery room and given a spinal block, and just after Penny's head appeared, I went to sleep. Sometime before noon, I was wheeled back to my room. I was still groggy when the phone rang.

"You have to come home right away, Mommy. It's an emergency," Kelly announced with characteristic theatricality.

"What's the emergency?" I asked with a certain maternal skepticism.

"Our new baby-sitter, Mechtild, is getting married, and there won't be anyone to take care of us," she told me.

"Kelly," I said, "Mechtild just arrived from Germany. Whom do you think she's going to marry?"

"Tom, my bus driver," she said. "She met him when he brought me home from school today, and he's going to call her tonight."

"Don't worry, Kelly," I reassured her. "You have a new baby sister, Penny, and we will both be coming home in a few days." (Kelly was right. She always knew what people were doing. Mechtild and Tom married a year later.)

Penny was a wonderful, easy baby, but our household was a chaotic nightmare. Brian ran—and fell—constantly. He caromed off the furniture, momentarily stabilized, then crashed, but he couldn't walk. He learned to throw himself out of his crib and playpen, but he couldn't stand without assistance. I installed a second, taller gate over the stairs to the basement after he propelled himself over the lower barrier. It seemed there was no safe place to put him. If he wasn't injuring himself, he was destroying all that came within his reach. Eventually, we installed an intercom system in the house and kept it on all the time, even at night, to keep track of Brian's peripatetic excursions. Even then, the surprises didn't stop.

Brian had finally gained confidence in the bathtub, allowing me to sit on the edge of the tub with one leg in the water. He was content to sit in the water and hold onto my leg with one hand while splashing water with the other hand. Slowly I had been able to increase the water level. However, by the time he was able to be bathed like the other children, I had a new problem. He wanted to swim, and keeping his head above water was a real problem. We went back to putting very little water in the tub.

By the time Brian had achieved some semblance of balance in walking and running, he spoke a lot of gibberish, which no one understood. Sometimes he would bring me a toy in an effort to illustrate what he meant. Sometimes he would fly into a rage, kicking and screaming when I asked him to repeat what he had said. Sometimes he didn't seem to understand what I said and that, too, would lead to outbursts of kicking and screaming. It was easy for strangers who saw him in a rage to shake their heads and mumble "spoiled" under their breath, but with three other children in the house, Brian didn't have much of a chance to become spoiled.

Together, Kelly and Brian required constant supervision, and even with supervision, they created tremendous messes. They had no interest in quiet activities or in climbing a jungle gym or sliding down a slide. They preferred climbing up bookcases or riding a wagon down a flight of stairs. Brian scaled a stack of drawers he had pulled from his dresser to reach a six-foot-high shelf. Kelly hung onto the medicine cabinet door and became frantic when it swung open and her feet no longer reached the sink. Brian pushed over furniture, and Kelly ran up and down the piano keys. Whitney watched the goings-on, participating when she deemed it safe. She, at least, seemed to have some idea of safety. I did my best to cope with my three older children while caring for infant Penny.

It wasn't that I didn't say No! It sometimes seemed that all I said was No! But neither Kelly nor Brian seemed to understand No! and subsequent punishments. Usually, after one bad scare, children don't do the same thing again. I still couldn't let go of Kelly's hand in the parking lot when I wanted to put the groceries in the car. She would run around without ever looking for cars even though she had narrowly missed being hit on several occasions. It scared her, but it didn't stop her.

I had always had plenty of energy. Now I was tired around the clock. I have to admit four children under six years of age could sap anyone's strength, but what really sapped my strength was a constant, nagging worry about Brian.

His lack of speech, incessant activity, and outbursts of kicking and screaming were constant reminders that something was not right. Perhaps the high fever I had had during the third month of my pregnancy had damaged him. I wished I hadn't gone on that trip to the Caribbean. I wished I wasn't so tired. I wished I could find some expert who would really listen to my worries and answer my questions.

When Brian was two, we were invited to the opening of the Century Plaza, a new hotel in Los Angeles, and we decided to take Kelly, Whitney, and Brian with us. We wanted the children to experience the new sights, smells, food, and cultures that travel affords. Although he still wasn't speaking intelligibly, I was determined that Brian would at least be able to say, "How do you do," and shake hands with anyone we might meet. So, several times each day, for day after day after day, we practiced introductions. I showed him how to knock on the door. Then I would open it and invite him in. I would introduce him to an imaginary visitor, whose part I played. We would practice shaking hands, and I would say, "How do you do?" Each time, I would have Brian try to repeat the words after me. Very slowly he mastered the words, and as he repeated them during our practices, I would tell him to look me in the eye as he spoke. I kept hoping his mastery of this phrase would lead to the mastery of other words, but it didn't. "Still," I said to Jay, "at least we know he can speak one sentence correctly for this one occasion, and he shakes hands beautifully."

When we arrived at the hotel in Los Angeles, we boarded the elevator with an acquaintance of Jay's who had never met me or our children. When it was his turn, Brian shook the man's hand, looked him squarely in the eye, and said, "How do you do in your eye?" You can imagine my mixed emotions as we got off that elevator.

It is never easy to travel with a two-year-old, but that trip to California really tested my fortitude. While we were there, Brian flew into a rage several times, once in the middle of the San Francisco airport. I had no idea why he was kicking and screaming, and every time I tried to pick him up, he screamed louder. People stared and made caustic remarks, mostly having to do with me. As I stood there feeling embarrassed, helpless, and incompetent, Brian suddenly ran off to see an antique car on display and returned with a big grin on his face. Successfully engaged, he was enchanting. But he was seldom successfully engaged.

The night we returned home, I was awakened by a loud crash and muffled crying. I dashed to the living room. There on the floor was Brian, beneath a mountain of books and adjustable shelves.

Two nights later a strange smell woke me around 3:00 A.M. I pulled myself out of bed and headed down the hall. Penny was sleeping in her room. Brian was awake and playing in the playroom adjacent to his room, a not unusual occurrence. I followed the smell to the kitchen, where I found Brian's stuffed animals baking in the oven. They were too hot to touch but had not yet burst into flames.

The following night I woke up at about the same time. The house was unusually cold, and the wind seemed to be howling both inside and out. The front door was wide open. In the moonlight I saw Brian, in his pajamas, making a snowman on the front lawn. I dashed out and carried him in. His feet and hands were like ice cubes. I soaked them in cold water until he was able to tolerate warm water. By the time I got him to sleep, it was time to make breakfast and help the girls dress for school.

Desperate, I called our pediatrician, Dr. Holburn, for advice. "What should I do about Brian at night?" I asked. "I'm afraid to go to sleep, and I feel all our lives are at stake."

Dr. Holburn said I should lock Brian in his room. I wasn't happy with the solution. I was not sure what emotional effect the restraint would have on him, and I had begun toilet training him. Locked in his room, he would not have access to a bathroom.

"Just lock the door and stop worrying," the doctor said.

So, for an entire year, I locked Brian in his room at night.

One morning I couldn't believe the smell and mess I encountered. At some point during the night, Brian had removed his diaper and made a large bowel movement in the middle of his rug. After climbing back into his diaper, he had mounted his tricycle and ridden it back and forth through the mess. I was furious, but how could I punish him when I was the one to blame for having locked him in his room, preventing him from getting to the bathroom even if he had wanted to get there?

Although my parents and friends listened to my concerns, they didn't know how to help. Dr. Holburn had no explanations for Brian's behavior or development. When I worried about Brian's lack of balance and his unintelligible speech, he pointed out that not all children develop at the same rate. When I spoke of his constant activity and his outbursts of rage, Dr. Holburn said he was a boy and he would outgrow temper tantrums.

I wanted to believe him, but I knew temper tantrums. Temper tantrums are the yelling and crying you have to put up with when you have said no to a second cookie a half hour before dinner. Brian's outbursts seemed to be born out of sheer frustration as he attempted to understand the world around him and to make it understand him.

Even my father found Brian difficult. The summer after Brian turned three, my father came for a visit. One day, he and Brian, riding his tricycle, went for a walk. Half an hour later, they returned, with my father frustrated and bewildered.

"Brian doesn't want to ride on the sidewalk," he announced. "He wants to ride over the flowers." When my father had told Brian he couldn't ride over the flowers, Brian had refused to go anywhere at all. Scolding and cajoling didn't work. Brian was furious. Finally my father had forcibly brought him home. After telling me the story, Dad remarked, "I wish Brian were a little less good looking and a lot easier to handle."

Brian was constantly running into things, fast and hard, getting bruised by furniture or doors, getting cut by breaking glass. In one three-week period, we took him to the hospital seven times: once for an EEG (which showed no abnormality), the other times for stitches to repair injuries to his head and wrist. Yet, neurologists, clinical psychologists, neuropsychologists, ophthalmologists, and otologists all told us Brian was fine, just very active.

The ophthalmologist said there was nothing wrong with Brian's eyes. The otologist found no deficiency in his hearing, and his electroencephalogram showed a normal brain scan. One doctor said that Brian was an "exceptional child," which I later discovered meant that he thought Brian was either brain damaged or emotionally disturbed. But that was as specific as any evaluation had been, and not very helpful. But if Brian was fine, why was it that the only safe way he seemed to be able to move around the house or outside was in play cars? He had several, which he propelled by foot. Although he bumped into anything and everything, he never got hurt because the sturdy front end of each car served as a blocker, opening a path and saving him from injury.

Even Brian's eating habits were bewildering. From the time he was a year and a half old until his fourth birthday, he craved orange juice. He had a good appetite, but he ate only two large meals each day, picking at the third one. It seemed that two meals were all he could handle, but there was no apparent consistency as to which meal he would just pick at. His behavior had nothing to do with what foods he liked, nor how much food he had eaten at the preceding meal. And chewing—he chewed forever. He would chew poultry and meat, including hamburger, endlessly, and it never seemed to go down. Eventually I would remove the dry mass from his mouth. At least in this case, I got a useful answer to my question. The dentist said Brian had a reverse tongue thrust. Having no time for tongue therapy, I gave Brian soft foods like mashed potatoes, soft peas, and applesauce, which he could swallow without a problem.

Worry, especially worry about your children, can make you do things you wouldn't normally do. One day I needed Dr. Holburn to review a report on some tests Brian had been given. When I got to his office, I found that the waiting room was filled. I'd had a particularly bad day but sat down obediently to wait my turn. More than two hours passed. I looked at my watch and realized I would soon be late for a car pool. Although there were still people ahead of me, the next time the door to the doctor's office opened, I rushed in. The doctor looked up from his desk and said, "Mrs. Hart, I can't see you now. I have to talk to the parents of a boy Brian's age who are awaiting their son's test results."

"I have to drive a car pool in just a couple of minutes," I protested, "and I, too, need you to discuss my child's test results."

"You will have to wait," he said, and he paused. "The fact is I have to tell those other parents that their son is dying of cancer."

I could barely get out of his office with my dignity intact and the tears held back.

I refused to believe there would be no answers for Brian, and I did my best to bury my worry deep inside me. I kept busy, very busy. I spent a great deal of time doing things with the children, and I made sure I had some time every day with each child alone. I staggered their bedtimes so as to give each child an exclusive half-hour. I made plans with friends who had children close in age to my own. When I watched other children who were Brian's age, I did not let myself think of how worried I was. I kept telling myself the doctors had to be right, but deep inside me I kept thinking something wasn't right.

As time went on, my feelings of loneliness and helplessness increased. I never seemed to have any time for myself or any person to whom I could turn. I tried to involve Jay with the children and to discuss my feelings with him, but Jay couldn't see that there was a problem. "If Brian does have a problem," he told me as I worried one evening, "it's your fault for not knowing how to raise a son."

In some ways during those early years, I became a robot, without emotion, except on those occasions when the dam broke, and the dam didn't always need a major catastrophe to break. One day after screaming at Kelly, I sat in my bedroom and cried. Why was Kelly always testing me? Why couldn't I stay in control of myself and be the mature, loving mother Kelly needed and I wanted to be? Why could neither Kelly nor Brian ever take no for an answer? Why did they keep doing and asking the same things over and over again?

A half-hour later, Kelly entered my room and asked if I had been crying. Embarrassed that she had so completely gotten me down, I lied and said no. Kelly left the room shaking her head, and I retreated to the bathroom. In the mirror I saw my eyes were very red and puffy. For sure I hadn't fooled Kelly, and now I had thrown another wrench into our relationship by lying to her. I knew Kelly was scared of me, that she never knew what would trigger a blow-up, but I didn't dare relax. If I relaxed, I would worry. If I relaxed for a moment, I was bound to find Kelly swinging in the tops of trees or Brian riding his surrey into the oil tank struts, leaving him injured and the house without heat.

3

Invited, but Not Invited Back

"Wanawidawuck."

—Brian

As the time approached for Brian to enter three-year-olds nursery school, I tried again to put some of my fears behind me and focus on his strengths. After Brian's initial interview (if "interview" is the right word for asking a child to play in front of someone), the school had made an exception in enrolling him. "His sisters are already going here," Miss Lock, the nursery school teacher, had said. "A lot can happen in a year. Maybe some of his difficulties will work themselves out."

Perhaps with some work, I thought, I could build Brian's confidence in some areas and direct his energy into activities that did not destroy the house. Although his sense of balance was dreadful, he could run, so we did a lot of running and climbing together. We worked on kicking and throwing soccer balls and basketballs. A punching bag in the basement let him work off steam in a nondestructive manner. I bought a hammer, large nails, and several large two by fours. Pounding nails into the two by fours also let him work off steam. Brian spent hours in the basement happily hitting his punching bag, hammering nails, and riding his surrey and wagon. He was always good at entertaining himself, but it was never safe to leave him alone or with one of his sisters. You never knew when he would get angry and throw the hammer or decide to chase one of his sisters and hit her with it or ride one of his vehicles into her, the furnace, or the hot water heater.

Now the days were filled with skills practice with Brian and general chaos. We had two baby-sitters, Ingrid and Barbara, who watched Kelly and Whitney and also did the laundry, cooking, and cleaning, while I dealt with Brian and kept an eye on Penny. I had other chores, of course, like keeping the house stocked with groceries and paying the bills, but such activities paled next to the attention Brian required.

More than anything, I wanted Brian to be able to handle nursery school. At the same time, I didn't want his teacher to give up in total despair as she dealt with him and the other three-year-olds in the class.

Brian's behavior often seemed to magnify everything that went on around him, even the inevitable clashes that occur between siblings. One day at snack time, Brian blew into his straw and splattered chocolate milk on Kelly. "That's not how you use a straw, you idiot! Now you've ruined my favorite blouse," she screamed at him. As I was washing the milk out of the blouse, I heard Penny start to cry. Brian had grabbed her cookie, and when she had tried to get it back, he had hit her. I sent Brian to his room, where he screamed for two hours. By dinner time Whitney had a headache, and so did I.

By the end of every day, I needed a vacation, but Brian did not seem to be tired. At night, after he was in his pajamas, he would wait for me on his bed, loudly propelling a miniature road-grader or dump truck through a terrain of blankets and pillows. He was so active that up to the very last instant of wakefulness he was on the move. Hours later, when making the rounds of the children's bedrooms before I went to bed, I often found him asleep draped over his night table or sprawled atop a pile of toy cars in his closet. He slept with his eyes half-open, as if watching me, as if keeping an uneasy eye on a world that must have seemed more an enemy than a friend. But, still, he slept. The question was, Was he ready for school?

That was September. The following March, after Brian had been in nursery school for six months, the question was answered. Miss Lock looked at me from across her desk and said, "I'm afraid we just can't offer Brian the right environment after all."

Miss Lock gazed down at Brian's folder, open in front of her, as though considering its contents for the first time. She and I were about the same age, but her plain wool sweater and severe hairstyle gave her a no-nonsense demeanor that could be reassuring or, as now, forbidding to parents.

Neither of us spoke. The roar of the March wind temporarily filled the silence. Ridge School was in Brookline, set down amid willow trees in a protective dell, a setting for which the wealthy Boston suburb is famous. In warm weather, the willow trees took the edge off the modern lines of additions to original residential structures. Nothing took the edge off now. The wind whipped the willow tendrils horizontal. Between patches of snow, the ground looked hard and unforgiving.

Miss Lock cleared her throat. We were at an awkward juncture. She was a sympathetic woman and undoubtedly what she had to say was painful for her, although not as painful for her to say as for me to hear. After all, Kelly and Whitney had already blazed a family trail through Ridge's nursery program, and Penny was scheduled to begin next year.

And Brian? To put it charitably, Brian had proved to be a challenge. The file in front of Miss Lock was a prop, an unnecessary aid to her memory. No teacher would ever forget Brian. Trying to control him, to keep and hold his attention, was like trying to hold water in an open hand. He still snatched cookies off other children's plates. He tried to flip the goldfish out of the aquarium. Story time, when the children lay quietly on their mats and the teacher read aloud *Rumpelstiltskin* or *Beauty and the Beast*, was often impossible with Brian. He dashed around the room overturning chairs or tables, smashing through the doll house or model garage. His sturdy forty-five-pound frame collided with anything that got in his way. Moreover, he was almost four years old and still wasn't toilet-trained; even Penny was ahead of him in this regard.

Furthermore, Brian's language skills were precarious at best. Sounds burst from his mouth in frantic, undecipherable explosions. He ran through the house saying, "Wanawidawuck, wanawidawuck" and other jumbled words that no one understood. Kelly and Whitney referred to my mother as Mama and my father as Papa. Brian called each of them what sounded like "Mamapapa." Buses were "pop" and all fruit, including bananas, he called "ball." If he asked for a "ball" and you guessed the wrong fruit, he flew into a rage on the spot.

Fortunately in the fall, when Jay and Dr. Holburn had pooh-poohed my fears that Brian had language problems, Miss Lock had backed me up. Recent practice with me had teased these knots of sound into strings of words that, although they might not make sense, were recognizable as language.

At least when *Air-we* disappeared, we knew what Brian wanted. Air-we was a red stuffed animal with no fur that Brian took to bed every night. As time passed, Air-we became smaller and smaller until only a tiny piece of material was left. Brian would clutch it in his pinky and accompanying finger, plug his thumb into his mouth, and eventually fall asleep. The night that the remnant of Air-we disappeared, Brian cried for two hours. We tore the house apart but to no avail. No other stuffed animals would do, and it was a long and difficult night. Six months later, Kelly found the remnant under the dining room rug and enthusiastically showed it to me en route to delivering it to Brian. I explained that Brian had grown up and could get along without *Harry* now, so Kelly reluctantly handed the piece of cloth over to me.

However, even I, Brian's mother and staunchest advocate, had to admit that his progress didn't put him on an equal footing with his playmates. Bursts of rage still followed on the heels of his frustrated attempts to make himself understood.

"Disruptive"—Miss Lock's word—hardly did Brian justice. Although technically Brian was scheduled for nursery school Monday through Friday from 8:30 to noon, he rarely lasted that long. The school would telephone: Brian had soiled his pants; Brian had stolen someone's snack; Brian refused to stop screaming; Brian had (a) broken, (b) bitten, (c) smashed, (d) thrown—take your pick—(1) another child, (2) himself, (3) toys, (4) furniture, (5) sand. The end result was always the same—a telephone call from the Ridge School secretary: "Mrs. Hart, this is Marcia. I'm terribly sorry to bother you, but could you come get your son? I'm afraid today doesn't seem to be a very good day for him."

Indeed, on a good day Brian lasted most of the morning. In a good week, he would make it through three full mornings. But if, for some reason, Miss Lock didn't have a classroom assistant whose efforts could be channeled almost exclusively into keeping watch over Brian, I was sure to get a call within an hour of dropping him off at the school. I can't recall a single time when he ever made it all the way from Monday to Friday without being asked to leave.

Miss Lock shifted uneasily behind her desk. She was a well-intentioned woman. Even so, as the injured party, or mother of the injured party, I wasn't about to make her job any easier. Under the present circumstances, I found it hard to resist the angry thought that maybe Ridge School made sure it didn't have the resources to handle children like Brian.

Miss Lock spoke. "We're just not prepared to handle Brian. Our play groups are too large to give him the care he needs. There are too many other children that also need to be taught and watched over."

I nodded. "So you're saying—?"

"Brian is welcome to finish out the spring, but we think he would benefit more by attending a different nursery program in the fall." She looked truly pained. When either Kelly or Whitney had had a problem, Miss Lock and I had communicated easily.

"If I were in your shoes, I'd look for a nursery school with small play groups, three or four other children, six at the maximum. Brian needs a lot of individual attention. I wish I had a nursery school to recommend," she added, "but I don't know of any that have such small play groups."

We stood up at the same time. Both of us knew I was upset, just as we knew that nothing either one of us could say would remedy the situation. I thanked her for trying to work with Brian.

"I know this is hard on you," she said. "But don't give up. Brian's bright, I'm sure of it—no matter what his problems are."

The wind howled again. "We'll find someplace for him," I said, sounding more confident than I felt. I thanked her for her advice and left. Outside I hugged myself against the cold.

❖ ❖ ❖

Brian was a puzzle. He "didn't add up." He rarely sat still, he spoke in phrases that you could barely understand, but once someone had helped him learn a word, he didn't forget it. He didn't seem to understand many of the things that were said to him, but he could work out with me in the basement gym, and he seemed to have a sense of humor. For instance, during the year, I had taken him to Dr. Rheingold, the head of neurology at Children's Hospital, for some further testing. It felt like one test too many to Brian. When Dr. Rheingold asked him to repeat the finger-nose test, Brian put his hands in his lap and told the doctor, "You quazy." Dr. Rheingold had said

Brian was hyperactive, but he had no other suggestions, and he had found no other problems.

Many parents first deny the truth when they learn their child has a handicap, then they bargain over the dimensions of the disability, and finally they accept the child as he or she is. For me, the denial stage was different. I knew there was a problem with Brian from the beginning; it was the people around me who did the denying. What I did deny from the beginning was the possibility that Brian would never live a self-sufficient, productive life. I knew he was a beautiful human being with tremendous potential. It might take work to let that potential flourish, but that didn't worry me. After all, my parents had taught me nothing important is achieved without effort, and without effort nothing at all is achieved.

I began my search for a new nursery school with a high teacher-to-student ratio by checking with Dr. Holburn and Dr. Rheingold. Both agreed that Brian would be served best by an environment in which he received much more attention than was possible in an ordinary nursery school, but neither of them knew of any such program. We canvassed our friends for suggestions, but they couldn't help us either.

With no suggestions from either the school or the doctors, and frantic to take some action, I was reduced to going through the Yellow Pages of the phone book. I asked a good friend, Betty Elliot, to help me. Betty and I had become acquainted shortly after the birth of Kelly. We had met as neighbors, pausing in the way that new parents will to compare children and baby carriages. Coincidentally, her first child had been born on the same day as Kelly. As we talked, we discovered that we shared similar midwestern backgrounds. Both of us felt friendless and at sea in Boston, and we both had husbands whose occupations kept them away for long workdays and some weekends. We had soon become friends.

We divided the alphabet in half. Betty, calling from her house, took *A* through *M*, and I started dialing all those nursery schools whose names began with the letters N through Z. I dialed all morning without any luck. "Me neither," Betty said when we took a break. "You'd think we were looking for a cure for cancer. Why don't we break for lunch and then pick things up later this afternoon?"

"I've got a couple more calls to make," I said, "then I'll be finished with the W's and can do the rest of the alphabet quickly after lunch." I dialed the number for a place called the Robert Wilder Children's Center. By this time I had pared my speech down to its bare-bones essentials, and I quickly outlined my problems. My son was difficult and disruptive, and I was looking for a nursery school that offered small play groups.

An administrator informed me that Wilder *specialized* in small play groups, usually no larger than three or four children. They would have to interview Brian and give him some tests to be sure he would fit into their program. The Wilder psychologists would also like to meet me and, eventually, Jay.

Ecstatic, I rang Betty right back. "I found a place!" I cried.

"Thank goodness. My fingers were about to fall off."

"They're going to interview Brian and give him some tests," I said. "The interview's in a week. Betty, I'm flying. I didn't think we were ever going to find a place."

"I don't want to be a party-pooper, but maybe we should keep calling—just in case things don't work out."

"It's going to work out," I said. "It has to."

4

A Slap in the Face

"It is our opinion that Brian is a severely emotionally disturbed little boy."

—Robert Wilder Children's Center psychologist

S ome dates are burned forever into my memory. One of them is Wednesday, March 16, 1966, the day of Brian's interview at the Wilder Center. That morning my thoughts raced alternately down two tracks: Please, please, please, let this be the right place for Brian, and What if they don't take him? Witnessing Brian's daily failure to thrive at Ridge had left me asking myself over and over again: Were we doing something wrong? How could we help him? So much of my attention was focused on Brian at that time that recent tests indicating that Kelly was learning disabled did not weigh on me particularly heavily. That, I thought, the school could handle, at least until I got Brian settled.

Brian shared my excitement on that morning when I told him that we were going to take a trip in the car to visit a new nursery school. He was fascinated with automobiles, and riding in the car always seemed to calm him down. After breakfast he ran to the coat closet, pulled on his winter jacket, and scampered down the back stairs to the car. His intelligent brown eyes sparkled, and a smile lit up his face. We got in the car. I paused with my hand on the key. "Ready?" I asked.

"Ready! Set! Go!" he cried. For the moment, with his toy dump truck clutched on his lap and with his chin up as he strained to see out the window, he actually resembled the angel that I had tried to convince Ridge School teachers really lived inside the frantic young boy in their care.

We backed out of the garage and started down the hill. I could never leave our Brookline home without thinking how much I loved it, or return to it without feeling a brief sense of peace, no matter what turmoil was affecting our family life. We were lucky to have a marvelous house on such a beautiful piece of property. Our home sat atop a rise reached by an access road that cut across a deep slope of landscaped lawn. In spring, rhododendrons and two-hundred-year-old lilacs transformed our yard into a perfumed bower of violet and pink. Wisteria and forsythia painted both sides of the drive with hopeful bands of violet and yellow.

The border between Brookline and Boston was only five minutes away by car, and the farther we drove, the more unreal our home seemed. At Washington Street we entered into the shadow of the elevated subway as it snaked its way down Washington Street into one of the city's poorest neighborhoods. Clichés of inner-city decline soon appeared to mark our progress away from home—graffiti, boarded-up storefronts, empty and derelict lots. The Wilder Center was located in an old neighborhood that time had ground into a modern slum. Stopping at intersections, I forced my gaze straight ahead, frightened of the forlorn men huddled on corners, bottles in brown paper bags passing from hand to hand. We lived among none of these things, and I was glad as we drove past them now that Brian was happily occupied with his dump truck. "Red!" he shouted at one point. "Red! Red!"

Fortunately, I happened to glance in the rear-view mirror just in time to see a red Mustang disappear. "That's right, Brian. I see the car, too."

His smile filled me with relief. If I had missed seeing the Mustang or had failed to pick out the proper red object (Quick, guess! The red-brick building? The red Coca-Cola advertisement?), Brian would have been in tears. He hated being misunderstood, and communication was still a precarious business.

Deep parallel ruts marked an ad hoc parking lot cut out of the yard at the Robert Wilder Children's Center. We bounced to a halt. I have no patience for people who read omens into every little happenstance, but it was difficult not to contrast the shabby aluminum siding of the old house that made up the Wilder Center with the pastoral serenity of Ridge School and not wonder what was happening to Brian. Wilder's windows were filthy, and paint flaked from the wooden eaves and casements. Instead of a neat lawn, there were broken bottles, old tires, and a shattered box spring floating in the sea of mud that surrounded Wilder. I dreaded going inside, but this was the only nursery school I'd found with six or fewer children to a play group, which everyone agreed was what Brian needed. Ignore the squalor, I told myself, Brian doesn't see it, and Brian is the reason you're here.

"We're here!" I cried with as much enthusiasm as I could muster.

Mothers of Wilder Center children filled a cavernous waiting room off the foyer. A bricked-over fireplace gaped cheerlessly at the worn furniture. A receptionist on the other side of the foyer took our names, and a moment later a woman in her early forties appeared wearing a white lab coat. "I'm Dr. Elizabeth Rosen," she said coolly. "I'll be seeing Brian today."

"If I can answer any questions—" I began, but she shook her head.

"Why don't we just see what we can learn from Brian? Would you mind waiting here?" she added in a way that said I was to stay behind.

She grasped Brian's hand and lead him down the linoleum-lined corridor that led through a set of double doors painted orange. As the doors swung open, an exhalation of institutional disinfectant blew out. Brian looked back at me over his shoulder. I smiled and waved goodbye to him as the doors swung closed. In time, after we had made many visits, the Wilder Center's physical decay and the atmosphere of resources stretched to the maximum would lose their power to shock me, but I would never be at ease with the staff's clinical coolness.

Taking the only unoccupied seat in the waiting room, an armchair upholstered in split Herculon, I pretended to read. The other mothers, who evidently knew each other, smoked and talked. From time to time a child would run into the foyer screaming, "Mommy! Mommy!" A teacher would soon appear to drag the child back. My insides churned as I raised my gaze over the top of my book to watch these desperately clinging children pulled firmly away from their mothers. Brian might have his problems, but behaviorally he seemed light years ahead of these children.

After forty-five minutes, Brian appeared with Dr. Rosen. She patted him on the head and smiled, an encouraging sign, I hoped. "I'd like to see him again," she said.

I agreed at once. "Did you want to ask me anything now?" I asked. After all, I had been observing Brian for almost four years now, it seemed to me I could offer some insights.

"Do you *want* me to ask you something?"

I fumbled, "I just thought—"

"That won't be necessary."

She didn't offer an explanation of her session with Brian, and not wanting to rock the boat, I didn't ask for an explanation. We drove straight from the center to Ridge School to pick up Kelly and Whitney. I took Brian by the hand as we went inside to fetch the girls. The orderliness of things assaulted me—clean, unmarred floors, freshly painted walls, and a rainbow of construction-paper letters pasted on the windows.

Brian seemed unaffected. In the car, Whitney said, "Where did you go today, Brian?"

"School! Saw Red!" he shouted triumphantly.

Three weeks later, Brian and I returned to Wilder for testing. I had learned in the interim that the Wilder Center was affiliated with Harvard, and I couldn't help hoping the tests would give us some answers for Brian. The diagnostician was a petite woman named Dr. Kane. Her blond hair was pulled straight back into a pony tail, and she had the same no-nonsense air as Dr. Rosen. All of us shook hands.

"We'll be going upstairs for the session today," she announced.

Brian held my hand as we followed her down the dark corridor, through the orange swinging doors and up two flights of stairs. Conditions on the third floor were no better than on the first. Paint flaked from ceilings mapped with water stains; ancient wallpaper blistered on corridor walls. The doors had knobs positioned a foot higher than normal. "So the children can't reach them," Dr. Kane said, observing my glance. It gave me an uneasy feeling, but at the same time, I understood, because I knew I couldn't leave Brian alone for a minute. My mind flashed to the week before, when I was folding laundry one day and listening through the intercom to Brian, who was playing with his blocks and trucks in the family room. I suddenly realized the room was very quiet— always a bad sign. I smoothed out the wrinkles on the shirt I was folding and headed towards the family room. As I passed through the kitchen, I heard Brian say, "I'm gonna bwake it." I increased my gait, and as I dashed into the family room, Brian said, "Bwoke it," and handed me the knobs off the TV. "Sarwe, Mommy." He had wanted to see what was inside the TV and had hoped the knobs would open it. (As the knobs were not the kind that could be slid back on, I took the TV and Brian to a repair shop. I took Brian along so he could see the insides of a TV and not try to get into one of ours again. Happily, it solved the problem.)

51

Having reached the end of the corridor now, we entered the testing room, a drab chamber with a desk, a bookcase holding toys and blocks, a couple of tables, and several chairs. I was directed to take a seat in a corner, close enough to assure Brian of my presence but far enough away not to distract him. To my surprise and pleasure, Brian willingly shifted his attention from me to Dr. Kane, even though I was seated only a few feet away. Following her instructions, he clambered onto a chair at a low table obviously designed for children. Subdued in the unfamiliar surroundings, he shuffled his feet slowly back and forth, while I prayed that his cooperative mood would last.

Dr. Kane explained to Brian that she would be giving him some tests and that he should at least try to do everything. He snatched up the pencil, his eyes glued to the test booklet as she folded it open to the proper page and told him what to do. His face stiffened with concentration as he labored to complete the first page.

I slumped back in my seat, feeling some of the trapped tension drain out of the muscles in my shoulders. Tension had become such an intimate part of my life that its presence never stirred my awareness; its absence did, as it did now. Around Brian, I was taut as a violin string, constantly vigilant, never sure exactly what he would do next, always waiting for the next explosion, the next tantrum, the next accident.

With my other children, I felt like an ordinary parent, wheeling through the usual emotions—love, pride, frustration, anger, expectation, and hope. But Brian was another story. Because it seemed that his successes were my successes, his failures were my failures, each day was an emotional roller-coaster—up one minute, down the next.

If only his development were normal, I thought. If he were different, maybe I would be different too, especially at home—less tense, less the ruthlessly efficient organizer, less the tyrant always making sure things got done. Without the responsibility of constantly caring for Brian I would have time for myself. I could do things I enjoyed. Suddenly I realized I was fantasizing about playing tennis. I hadn't picked up a racket since I was pregnant with Brian. What had happened to the carefree girl who had once played varsity tennis for Sarah Lawrence? A stab of guilt drew me back into the present. I sat up in my chair, willing Brian to do well.

Halfway through the session, Dr. Kane opened the booklet to a picture of a man who was missing a leg. "Brian, this man is missing a leg. Can you draw one for him?"

Brian bowed his head over the picture. He quickly sketched a leg in the upper left-hand corner of the page. He grinned up at Dr. Kane as he handed over the booklet. She accepted the test booklet without comment and flipped through the pages until she came to a series of three mazes. "I want you to trace a way out of this maze," she said, putting her finger on the first and easiest one. Brian's pencil wound its way out of the puzzle without a second's hesitation. Dr. Kane again took the test booklet and began to skip ahead to the next test, but Brian snatched the booklet out of her fingers. He riffled back through the pages until he found the page he wanted and completed the two remaining mazes before she could stop him.

I was so proud of him I could hardly keep my seat.

"That's not necessary, Brian," Dr. Kane said. He looked at her as if to say, "Ha! Didn't think I could do that, did you!"

After the last test, Dr. Kane told Brian he could get down from his chair and go play with the blocks and toy cars in the corner of the room. Always a fan of anything having to do with cars, Brian jumped down from his seat, leaving us alone to talk.

The psychologist flipped through the booklet quickly, totting up Brian's results. My attention pricked up when she glanced at Brian's drawing of the leg and frowned. I waited for her pencil to add a small jot, an indication that Brian received credit for his answer, to the column of marks on the paper in front of her. Instead, she turned the page. I let her finish with the scoring before I asked questions.

"What," I wanted to know, "was wrong with Brian's leg drawing?"

"He didn't attach the leg to the man."

"But you didn't ask him to attach it. You just asked him to draw it."

"Normal children," she said in a slow, exasperated voice, as though I couldn't possibly have had any familiarity with such rarefied creatures, "attach the leg without being asked."

Okay, I thought. Sorry I asked. But what about Brian's leaping ahead to the more difficult mazes, why had she passed over them? Didn't his effort count for something?

"Those tests are for older children," she said when I queried her.

Obviously, we were operating from different perspectives. I saw intelligence and determination; she saw—I didn't know what she saw. What did his performance mean? Had she tested other children who responded like Brian? Could he be taught to behave differently? Why couldn't he sit still or master toilet-training? Why was he always crashing into things?

Dr. Kane only blinked at me. "As the tests clearly indicate, his behavior's abnormal. We'll call you when we've completed our full evaluation of his test results." End of discussion.

Of course his behavior is abnormal! I wanted to scream. That's why we're here! Brian stared at me in confusion as I hurriedly bundled him back into his winter coat and we made our way back down to the first floor without further diagnostic assistance. I was baffled and angry.

Later that night, after all the children were tucked in bed, Jay and I discussed my reactions to Brian's second session at the center. I had given up trying to get Jay to share his thoughts and feelings with me. I had known when we married that he expressed his feelings poorly, that something frightened him about letting others get close to his innermost thoughts and emotions. (The first time Jay invited me to visit for the weekend, he suggested I take a Saturday morning train to Boston from New York's Grand Central Station, which would give us only part of Saturday and Sunday together. Instead, I planned to fly up to Boston Friday evening. When he fumbled out some excuse about not being able to meet me at Logan airport, we agreed that I would take a cab from the airport and meet him in town. Only later did I learn that my flight time had coincided with his standing Friday evening session with his therapist. I've often thought this inability to tell me about his standing appointment simply previewed our later married life.) Rather naively, I had thought that time and love would unlock the shell Jay kept around himself. Instead, the demands and responsibilities of marriage, work, and children only drove him deeper into himself. Still, I did expect him to lend a hand in helping Brian overcome his problems.

After dinner we carried our glasses of wine into the playroom adjacent to the dining room. Of all the rooms in our house, the playroom was the one that symbolized "family" to me. Floor-to-ceiling cabinets for games and toys covered one wall. Another wall of windows looked out over the terrace. There was a television, a fireplace, and the indestructible Mexican tiles on the floor that could stand up to kids. One of Brian's pedal-powered cars, as dented and bruised as a veteran tank, sat in front of the fireplace, strangely inert without its driver.

Jay listened to my account of what had occurred in the session at the Wilder Center, but instead of sharing my frustration at their diagnosis of "abnormal behavior," he simply nodded. "I don't think you're giving them a chance," he said. "For heaven's sake, they're from Harvard, aren't they?"

"But we already know his behavior is abnormal," I said.

"Let's see what else they have to say before we jump to any conclusions." He took a sip of his wine. "I know if I were in their shoes, I'd sure hate it if every parent who came along with a problem kid tried to second-guess me. Look, they promised us a full evaluation, right?"

I conceded that this was correct.

"Good, let's see what they have to say then." He swallowed the rest of his wine in a gulp. "I'm going to bed. It's been a long day and I've got an early meeting. I'm sure they know their business."

Jay marched off with such an air of conviction that I wondered if somehow all my doubts were exaggerations. A moment later I heard the distant thrum of water as Jay showered. I dimmed the lights in the playroom and sat by myself, trying to make sense of my feelings and what I knew about Brian just from living with him.

Jay rose at 7:00 A.M. every morning. He shaved, dressed, and bounded down the long hall from our bedroom to the kitchen. Technically, I suppose he could claim to have breakfast with the children, since they were at the table, but they had long since learned not to interrupt him when he was reading the newspaper—and he always read the newspaper during breakfast. At night, I could pretty much count on hearing Walter Cronkite signing off on the seven o'clock news with "And that's the way it was, April 7, 1966, in the world tonight," before recognizing the rumble of Jay's car as it pulled into the garage.

Except for emergencies, Jay never had to deal firsthand with the confusion Brian could cause. I tried to keep Brian from hurting himself, anyone else, or too much of the furniture as he rocketed about the house, but he was always banging himself on the edge of a piece of furniture or crashing his hand through a window or breaking the glass covering the pictures in his room. Each time he was hurt, he panicked. The pain, the blood, the trips to the hospital terrified him. Without this experience, Jay simply couldn't understand how much I needed those few hours each morning when Brian was in nursery school and Penny was the only child at home. Family life for Jay involved a little television or an occasional game with the children between homework and bedtime. Preoccupied with his own therapy or with work, and often absent, he didn't realize how unmanageable life would become for us without a solution to Brian's problems. But, was Wilder a solution for Brian? Could they really help him?

The thought of having to care for Brian full time opened an abyss of anxiety in me. There wasn't enough of me to go around, even with all the help that money could buy. How would I care for our other children? Yet, at the same time, I dreaded handing Brian over to the care of psychoanalytic technicians like Dr. Kane or Dr. Rosen, who didn't see the sweet, intelligent little boy I knew was inside him. The word "abnormal" flitted like a bat through my dark thoughts.

❖ ❖ ❖

Wilder notified us in the first week in June that they had come to a conclusion. Could we please come in for a conference? Jay and I went together.

Dr. Rosen, Dr. Kane, and Jay and I sat in an empty conference room on the third floor. Dr. Rosen did most of the talking, with an occasional nod to Dr. Kane. I had to bite my tongue when she once again repeated the scores from Brian's second session and again commented on the abnormality of his behavior. She folded her hands, regarded us evenly, and finally gave us the conclusion. "It is our opinion that Brian is a severely emotionally disturbed little boy."

The skin on my face stung as if I had been slapped. Disturbed. Emotionally disturbed. Severely emotionally disturbed. Abnormal was okay, not great, but okay. Abnormal was almost the same as eccentric, and eccentric could also mean clever. No such escape hatch existed with severely emotionally disturbed. Dr. Rosen continued talking, but I didn't hear her. My mind was in flight. Was she saying that Brian was mentally ill? If so, did it follow that we, his parents, had made him that way? Jay had been in therapy of one kind or another for as long as I had known him, so I wasn't a complete stranger to the idea that emotional problems could cause behavioral difficulties, but I had never suspected that emotional problems might be the source of Brian's difficulty.

No one at Wilder, then or later, specifically said that Brian's behavior was due to my mishandling of him. It wasn't necessary. In effect, their diagnosis laid the blame at my feet. In Boston in the 1960s, the most favored perspective in the treatment of disturbed children was a psychoanalytic one. The influence of a child's mother, according to this outlook, was the all-important determinant in the child's mental health. In its extreme forms, psychoanalytic theory ascribed everything from autism to reading problems to the malign influence of the mother. Somewhere along the line, it would seem, I had gravely erred as a mother.

I sat stunned while the psychologists outlined their recommendations. Brian's treatment at the Wilder Center would involve two components: classwork and therapy. By attending small play groups two days a week, Brian, it was hoped, would acquire the social and intellectual skills that had eluded him thus far. He would also have therapy sessions with a staff psychologist.

"We would also like both of you to enter therapy with our staff members," Dr. Rosen said. "We think this is the most effective way of dealing with the family's problem."

Psychotherapy for everyone, all with the aim of getting at the root of whatever warped family dynamic had hurled Brian off the track of normalcy in the first place. Jay seemed unfazed. I mutely nodded my agreement. The center also insisted that Brian attend the Spencer Summer Day Camp, a local camp specifically designed for emotionally disturbed children, before school began. Then, in the fall, while Brian was at the Wilder Center, I would have to be available in the waiting room in case he or a staff member needed me.

I left Wilder in a state of shock. Could it be that the Wilder Center possessed a keener insight into my son—and for that matter, my effect on him—than I did myself? I would have been the last person to say that Brian was well-adjusted, but to call him emotionally disturbed did not seem to explain his problems either.

Jay, of course, disagreed. We argued as we drove home.

"They never once told me their program was just for emotionally disturbed children," I said. "I'm not sure that Brian is. I'm not sure what 'emotionally disturbed' means, for heaven's sake! They didn't even explain that!"

"What did you think their program was for? You saw those other kids—did their behavior look normal to you?" He shook his head. "You only see what you want to see. You're the one who's always asking, 'What's wrong with Brian? Why does Brian do this or that? What can we do about Brian?' Well, finally somebody comes along who thinks they know the answers, and you want to back off. I say, let's give them a try."

Our pediatrician, Dr. Holburn, made the same argument as Jay, although not as harshly. "No one's blaming you," he told me. "You're overreacting. Put Brian's interests ahead of your doubts. What have you got to lose? I'm sure he'll be fine at Wilder, and a summer at camp with emotionally disturbed children won't do him any harm. Besides, you're going to have to send him someplace—you look exhausted."

I seemed to have no other choice. My intuition predicted disaster, but in the end I acquiesced.

5

The Long, Hot Summer

"Brian! Stop! It's okay. Just tell me what's wrong."

—Nancy

My strongest support, as I argued that Brian was not emotionally disturbed, came from an old friend in Spain, Cristina Lana, a remarkable teacher who at one time had been imprisoned by the Franco regime. After her release, she had started a one-room school. As a junior in college, I had studied in Madrid for a year and was one of two boarders in Cristina's three-bedroom apartment. The rent we paid her, along with tuition from her students, helped support her school, which eventually ran from nursery school through high school and became one of Madrid's most prestigious institutions. Although she was old enough to be my mother, Cristina and I soon became fast friends. Among other things, I was awed by her intuitive rapport with children.

After my return to the United States, we had continued to keep in touch. We wrote often and spoke by phone once or twice a year, but I had never mentioned my difficulties with

Brian. Now, feeling trapped, I telephoned her. At the sound of her voice, I burst into tears. She waited while I regained control of myself. "Oh, Cristina, it's Brian. Something's not right. In fact, it's terribly wrong, and nobody seems to know what it is. I think I'm going crazy with worry."

"*Díme,*" she said in Spanish, "Tell me." I poured out my heart to her, delirious with relief at finding a sympathetic listener. Concluding my monologue, I said, "He isn't talking the way most four-year-olds talk, Cristina, and he doesn't seem to understand when you explain to him how to do something. But if you show him how to do it, he can do it."

Cristina then questioned me in detail about Brian's behavior for more than an hour. At the end of our conversation, she had no startling insights or easy solutions, but, like me, she doubted whether Brian's primary problem was an emotional disturbance. She urged me to keep Brian around normal kids, at least part of the time.

"At each stage of their development, children learn specific things from their peers," Cristina said. "They learn to share, to take turns, to get their way without hitting or kicking. It may not be evident now, but Brian may be picking up things from his playmates at Ridge. He may be more aware than you think. Maybe the Wilder Center looks like your only alternative, but that doesn't mean Brian has to spend all his time around disturbed children. Why not alternate his days at Wilder with days when he spends time with normal kids?"

It seemed to me this idea had merit even if it didn't answer all my questions. To date, I had intuitively resisted the Wilder diagnosis, but it was the only diagnosis I had. Okay, I was willing to compromise. If Wilder thought it could help Brian, I would give it all the assistance I could, short of segregating him from children who were not considered disturbed. The same day that I signed Brian up for the fall session at Wilder, I also enrolled him in the fall session at Green Acres Day School in Waltham, a town west of Boston. I had checked out Green Acres carefully and talked to parents who had sent their children there. The school's headmistress, Grace Mitchell, had suggested I read *Dibs in Search of Self* by Virginia Axline in order to understand the concept of emotional disturbance in children. I read the book, but to my thinking, Dibs, the disturbed young boy in the story, didn't resemble Brian in the least. Still, the warm environment and lush green lawns of Green Acres offered a welcome counterpoise to the clinical detachment and squalor that reigned at Wilder. I also liked the school's policy of enrolling one handicapped child in every class of normal children in the belief that all the children benefitted from the interaction. Against the Wilder Center's advice, Brian became the handicapped child for his class at Green Acres.

Unfortunately, Brian's summer would not be as well balanced. He would go only to Spencer Summer Day Camp, but at least he would also continue speech therapy. Speech therapy had become the bright spot. Shortly after my unhappy meeting with Miss Lock in March, and just before Brian's fourth birthday, Dr. Holburn had referred Brian to Gertrude Wyatt, director of psychological and speech therapy services in Wellesley, Massachusetts. Dr. Wyatt felt that Brian's behavior was due partly to frustration resulting from poor communication. She recommended a speech therapist, Lois Scott, whom Brian began seeing once a week.

Dr. Wyatt also suggested that Brian and I make a scrap book, using pictures from magazines to show familiar things. Each page of the scrap book would have only one picture. On one occasion, for instance, we put a picture of a cow on a left-hand page and a barn on the facing page, but we never put a cow and a barn on the same page. Looking at more than one picture and hearing more than one word at a time seemed to overwhelm Brian. After the pictures were in place, I pointed to the cow and said, "cow" and told Brian to repeat what I had said. Then I pointed to the barn and repeated the process.

Once I took an apple into Brian's room and asked him, "What is this?" while handing him the apple. Next I said, "apple" and had him repeat it. Then I had him eat a piece of the apple. Finally, I told him to find the picture of the apple in his scrap book. When he did, I again said, "apple" and had him repeat it just as I had said it. Brian and I played different versions of this game several times a day, usually for five or ten minutes.

It seemed to me that whenever Brian could touch something, he could learn it. Within three months of beginning his weekly sessions with Lois Scott and our own three-times-a-day sessions, more than half of what Brian said could be understood by everyone. Of course, he didn't use complete sentences, and sometimes he inverted the word order or the sounds of some letters, but still he didn't fly into rages quite as frequently. By the time he entered Wilder in the fall, he was no longer running around the house saying phrases like "Wanawidawuck." Instead he said fairly clearly, "I want to ride a truck."

When Spencer Summer Day Camp began, I took turns in a car pool with two mothers whose four-year-old sons were also signed up for camp. Aside from my brief observations of the children in the Wilder Center waiting room, driving these boys to Spencer was my first experience with children who were "emotionally disturbed," a grab-bag term that I came to learn stood for anything from mild depression to schizophrenia.

On my car-pool mornings, I picked up the boys at their houses and dropped them off at a large parking lot at the camp's entrance, where their counselors waited for them. At the end of the day I returned to the parking lot to collect the boys. Spencer's rules strictly forbade parents communicating with their sons' counselors or entering the camp grounds, even after the campers had departed for the day. I felt like a prison driver handing juvenile inmates to anonymous guards. It was the first of many reminders over the years of how dreadfully vulnerable the parents of troubled children become. So desperate are we to help our children that we endure any humiliation, tolerate any denial of our own insights, in order not to jeopardize our children's acceptance into a facility that holds out the hope of treatment. Don't talk to your child's counselor, you might contaminate the therapeutic experience. Don't try to argue with a professional evaluation, your observations can't compete with those of "the experts." Implicit in all of this is the assumption that you, the parent, have somehow failed and must now turn over the reins to those who "truly" understand your child's problem and its treatment.

Daniel, the son of a Brookline policeman, sat alone on his front steps each morning, waiting for us to arrive. A handsome, well-mannered boy, he got in the car without coaxing, sat still during the twenty-minute trip, and chatted amiably with Brian and me the whole way. Whatever diagnosis qualified him for Spencer was a mystery to me.

Terry, tall and thin for his age, had to be pushed into the car by his mother or another person each morning. He stared out the car window with a silent, catlike vigilance. "What are you looking for?" I asked, but he never could tell me. Our route took us past a two-story brown house several blocks from his home. As we pulled even with the house, he began to scream and make shrill, unintelligible noises. The third or fourth time this happened, I telephoned his mother to ask if something had happened to her son in that house.

"I don't know what you're talking about," she said. "We drive by that house all the time and Terry behaves just fine."

Eventually I changed our route and drove a half-mile out of our way just to avoid triggering a fit of hysterical screaming. During Terry's fits, Brian and Daniel would fall silent, clench their teeth, and stare ahead, refusing to look at Terry, waiting for the screaming to end. I tried to strike up a conversation with Terry's mother on several occasions, but if I mentioned the camp or Terry or anything that related to Brian's own problems, her gaze began to slide sideways, and she soon made some excuse to break off the discussion.

I had hoped that my contact with these boys and their parents would put a face on the label, help me begin to reduce the abstractions of psychoanalytic psychology into concrete knowledge that could be used to benefit Brian. Instead, I only ended up more baffled and frustrated. It was unnerving and depressing.

The first day Brian came home from Spencer, he slammed through the door into the kitchen and stormed past me. The energy that animated Brian at any given moment originated from any of several sources. The first was hyperactivity. Brian physically operated at high pitch. He needed to move, to be involved in activities that burned off that energy. The second source seemed connected to his frustration over his inability to understand others or make himself understood. The third source seemed to be related to difficulty he experienced in accomplishing certain tasks. No matter what the cause, there were times when Brian just seemed to get caught up in the momentum of his own physical storm, racing about the house, yelling and screaming, hitting anything within reach, including me. Since it was often difficult, if not impossible, to determine immediately the cause, the most efficient—and safest—way of dealing with him was to hold him. As I held him, I would force him to look at me and explain, or at least try to explain, what was wrong.

That afternoon, I grabbed for him, missed, then collared him on my second try. As he tried to wrestle out of my hug, I asked him what had happened. By way of an answer, he hurled his lunch box across the kitchen. "Brian! Stop!" I held him close until his struggles began to fade. "It's okay," I said over and over, "just tell me what's wrong." Slowly his body relaxed against me. Tears welled up in his eyes and dampened my shoulder, but he wouldn't speak.

At dinner it was the same thing. Kelly, Whitney, and Penny bantered as usual around the table, but Brian said nothing. At bedtime, when he still hadn't spoken a word, I went into his room and rubbed his back. "Why won't you speak to me?" I asked. The muscles of his back and shoulders hardened obdurately, and he buried his face in the pillow. Finally he fell asleep, but he never spoke to me.

The same thing happened the next afternoon.

That evening I telephoned the camp director several times, but he never returned my calls. I was getting desperate; Brian's behavior frightened me. Two days of camp had metamorphosed him from speaking relatively intelligibly to a silent, angry little boy. I debated whether or not to call Alan, Brian's counselor, at home. Although I knew Alan's name, camp policy dictated that we could do no more than wave at each other when I arrived to drop off or pick up Brian and his fellow campers. To call Alan would be such a flagrant violation of the rules that Brian might be asked to leave, and that, in turn, could jeopardize his entry into Wilder in the fall.

I paged through the telephone book, uncertain I could locate him, telling myself I was only looking up his number in case of an emergency. To my surprise, I found only one listing under his last name. I carefully recorded it in the little black book of numbers I always carried with me. But wait, I thought. Shouldn't I verify that it was, in fact, the correct number, just in case I really did need it for an emergency? I gave a mental shrug. Oh well, in for a dime, in for a dollar. I dialed the number, and when a women's voice answered, I asked to speak with Alan. I heard her calling him. Should I hang up?

"Hello," Alan said.

A vision of Brian hurling his lunch box across the kitchen rose in my mind. "Alan, this is Nancy Hart, Brian's mother."

"Ye-es?" he said warily.

"I know you're not supposed to talk to me, but something awful is happening to Brian. The last two days have been terrible. I've tried to reach the director, but he won't return my calls."

The telephone receiver became slick with sweat from my palms as I pleaded with this teenager to tell me what Brian did at camp, to describe his playmates.

Alan spoke in a hushed voice. I could hear his parents

conversing in the background. "I need this job for college money. If the director learns about this, he'll fire me."

I described how I'd spent the last several months teaching Brian to speak intelligible English, how he had moved from gibberish to communication, how his behavior had improved because he was no longer constantly frustrated with others' inability to understand him. Now he was coming home in a rage, refusing to tell me what was wrong. "I promise I won't tell the director we've spoken," I said, and I meant it.

Alan had been assigned to Brian and another little boy, who was also four years old. "This kid never talks—I don't know why. Brian spends the entire day trying to talk to him, but the kid never answers." He sighed. "I can't get him to talk either."

The campgrounds were fairly large, Alan explained, and so the pairs of campers were isolated for most activities. "Brian doesn't have much of a chance to play with other kids." He sounded apologetic. "Just that one boy."

I was shocked. This was a camp, a place for children to play together even as they worked on their problems. How could Brian ever learn to interact with other children if he was with only one child, especially a child who didn't speak? How could he practice talking if his partner didn't talk? I thanked Alan for speaking with me and said, "Don't get worried when you see me talking to the director on Monday morning. I'm going to insist that he place Brian with another child, but I'll tell him that I got the whole story from Brian."

Monday morning I drove Brian to camp and stayed until the director reluctantly met with me and agreed to change Brian's playmate. Never again that summer did Brian return home refusing to speak, but speech did not make that summer any easier.

It seems to be a basic fact of life with children that you no sooner solve one problem than another crops up. Once Brian could speak relatively intelligibly, we had a new type of communication problem. Often I understood his words but not what they meant. When this happened, he would toss himself around on the floor, screaming and kicking at everything.

One afternoon when he arrived home, he said, "I ride boat today down the grass."

"Were you on a boat that went through some grass in the water?" I asked.

"No," Brian responded with annoyance. "Boat goes on grass, not water."

I was totally bewildered, but I'd learned from experience that the best way to handle this kind of situation was to have Brian show me what he meant. We drove back to camp.

The first few afternoons that we had returned to the camp to discover what Brian meant, I had worried that I would run into the director. After all, I knew I was breaking one of the camp rules. Fortunately, the minute the campers left, the staff, including the director, also left, and I never saw anyone.

When we returned that particular day, Brian showed me a small, plastic boat at the top of a grass-covered hill. With a running start, he pushed the boat, jumped in, and sailed down the hill. When he reached the bottom, he came running back, took my hand, and pulled me to the swimming pool, which he pointed at, and said, "Water, no boat. Boat goes on grass, Mommy, not water." He was right, of course. Thank heavens I hadn't insisted he was wrong.

As the summer progressed, I found Brian usually came home tense and upset from camp, so I frequently called Alan at home in the evenings to ask what had gone on that day. He would reluctantly tell me. Eventually he told me, "Look, before the first day of camp this summer, I had never had any experience with children, normal *or* emotionally disturbed, and the camp did not train us."

It made me frustrated and angry that a camp that supposedly helped children was, in fact, staffed with untrained personnel who were not even properly supervised. We were paying for a camp that was not helping Brian and that I feared might be damaging him further.

I wanted summer camp to end.

6

From the Frying Pan into the Fire

"I earnestly suggest you consider institutionalizing him."

—Dr. Sims

Camp finally did end, but the remainder of the summer did not prove any more peaceful. We did go on a family vacation before school started. We stayed in a house that was near the ocean and also had its own pool. Across the busy street in front of the house was a large hotel. Our vacation setting was a veritable mine field for Brian. If he wasn't watched every minute, I knew he might disappear in the ocean, drown in the pool, or be hit by a car, so I usually kept all the doors locked when he was inside.

One day my brother-in-law Roy drove up outside and honked the horn. When I opened the kitchen door, he called through his car window, "Are you missing something?"

"No, I don't think so," I replied.

"Well, how about this?" He stepped from the car and pulled Brian out behind him—soaking wet and reeking of scotch whiskey.

Somehow, Brian had gotten out without my noticing. He had either fallen in the pool or, after crossing the street, had sat in the hotel sprinkler system before romping through the hotel's lounge where people were dancing. Evidently thirsty after his adventures, he had polished off a few scotches that had been left unattended by some dancers. Brian's uncle had discovered him in the nick of time. It was definitely time for school, I thought then, despite my qualms about the Wilder Center.

Finally, school started. Brian would go to Wilder two mornings a week, and to Green Acres the other three days. I arranged my schedule so that I could sit in the center's waiting room each morning he was in his Wilder class, and I saw a psychologist, as the center required, for forty-five minutes during one of the two mornings I waited for Brian.

The center's waiting room had large, grimy windows with no curtains and an empty fireplace. A dilapidated sofa and chairs with extruding stuffing and springs were pushed against the room's curved walls. It was impossible to read or to concentrate on anything because the children constantly ran in and out of the waiting room and climbed onto their mothers' laps, where they remained until a teacher retrieved them. "I want my mommy," they screamed as the teachers dragged them down the hall and back into the classroom. Brian came to me only once. A classmate had broken his toy car, and his teacher had been unable to repair it. I bent the sides back into shape so they didn't interfere with the wheels' movement and handed the car back to him. "Thanks, Mom," he said and ran back to his classroom.

During the mornings, I talked to the other mothers and listened to stories about their children. We were all overwhelmed by our handicapped children, but, unlike me, these women seemed resigned to their youngsters' situations. I was determined to change Brian's behavior, and listening to stories about problems without solutions just made me more impatient.

The psychoanalytic method in vogue in the 1960s stressed secrecy. Parents were not allowed to talk to their child's

72

teacher nor to any psychologist other than their own. Once a term, however, both fathers and mothers all attended a group conference. Even at these sessions, you could talk only to your own psychologist. If you wanted to say something to someone other than your psychologist, you were expected to direct your comments to your psychologist, who would then repeat the exact words to the person to whom the comments were addressed. This struck me as ridiculous, so during our second session, I said that I would speak to whomever I wished and I didn't want anyone to repeat what I had said. The psychologists looked at one another but didn't comment on my abrupt pronouncement. From then on our group sessions resembled a normal conference.

During the group conference and in my individual conferences, I asked repeatedly why Brian usually left class agitated and angry, but no one ever told me why, and I was not allowed to observe Brian in class. One day, to find out, I stood by the partially open classroom door and peeked in. The teacher's back was to me. Brian and two other children were seated at a table that held a pitcher of juice and a plate of cookies. The teacher was trying to get another child to join them. Suddenly the child ran to the table, climbed onto a chair, and stepped onto the table. He picked up the pitcher of juice and poured it over the heads of the seated children. Brian grabbed him, pulled him off the table, and slugged him. As I stood there longing to enter the room, another teacher came down the hall, closed the classroom door, and reminded me that mothers were to stay seated in the waiting room. I returned to the waiting room worrying that Brian would be punished for hitting the boy who had poured juice on him. What, I wondered, was Brian learning?

That question bothered me so much during that fall that I began trying to teach Brian at home, which meant that every day I sat down and tried to figure out how to get him to understand some of the concepts—"less" and "more," "big" and "small"—that most four-year-olds seemed to grasp easily.

From observing Brian, it seemed to me that he needed to handle things to understand concepts, so our nightly sessions
were filled with paper plates, cups of different sizes, and toy
cars, which he loved. To get him to understand "under" and
"behind," we hid under and behind boxes. At the end of each
session, after Brian had brushed his teeth and climbed into
bed, I would give him a back rub. He would slowly fall
asleep, exhausted, and I would sit there beside him for a few
minutes with my hands on his back, feeling him at rest, if not
at peace. At last, I would turn out his light and go to
Whitney's room. Invariably, I was late getting there for our
private half-hour visit, but unlike her sister Kelly, Whitney
never complained about my tardiness.

It was working, but it took time and energy to plan each
session with Brian.

My sessions with the Wilder psychologist were equally as
frustrating as sitting in the waiting room. Once a week I went
to the third floor office of Jane Vail. Jane was exactly my age,
and we soon discovered we had mutual friends from college.
She would move her chair from behind her desk so we could
face each other as we talked. She was easy to be with, and I
hoped that our conversations would help me to better understand and deal with my child, but they didn't. Jane could not
explain why Brian was in constant motion, to the point of
endangering himself, why he was always running into things
and hurting himself, or why speaking in complete sentences
seemed to be so difficult for him.

Finally, the week before Christmas, I began our session by
telling Jane that I liked her a lot. "The problem is," I said, hoping not to hurt her, "I don't know any more now than I knew
before our first meeting." I had analyzed with her my relationship with all of my children, my children's relationships
with each other, my relationship with my husband, my relationship with each of my parents, my parents' relationship
with each other, my husband's relationship with each of our
children, and his relationship with his parents—and none of

this had shed any light on Brian's problems. This litany of analyses would have been funny, except that I was desperate.

As I talked on, I reminded Jane that I had kept her up to date on everything Brian had done. "You're a wonderful listener," I said, leaning back in my chair to get the sun out of my eyes, "but I don't feel our sessions are helpful."

Jane stood to lower the shade behind her and then sat facing me again. Even though I didn't believe Brian needed me at the center, I continued, I was willing to be there. But I had bills to pay, mail to read, correspondence to take care of, and appointments to make. At the same time, every day I sat down and tried to figure out how to teach Brian a new skill. Plus, I had a husband and three other children who needed me. "If you really want to help," I told her, "please get me an office with a telephone that I can use the two mornings I'm here waiting for Brian." Jane said she would see what she could arrange when school resumed in January.

Over the year-end holidays, we took Brian, Kelly, Whitney, and Penny skiing. By the time we had reached the slopes, put Penny in the day care, and enrolled Kelly and Whitney in a ski class that first morning, Brian had lost his mittens. He seemed oblivious to the cold and wanted to go up on the lift with me. Over his protests, he and I started back to the cottage to get some new mittens. Fortunately, before we had gone all the way back, I found his mittens in the snow. With these in place, we rode the T-bar together to the first station. After we got off, I said, "Wait. I want to ski you down between my legs." I let go of his hand for a minute and bent over to adjust my bindings. When I stood up, he was gone, and I heard him screaming, "Help, Mommy, help!" He was fifty yards in front of me, headed straight down the mountain with no idea how to stop. Sheer luck allowed me to overtake and grab him before he fell or crashed into someone.

Brian's return to school, even the Wilder Center, seemed something of a relief. Moreover, when I arrived for my first session with Jane after vacation, she told me that I had an office with a phone in it. I was thrilled. To be sure Brian knew where he could find me if he needed me, we went to the center early the next day and he saw where I would be, but he never once came to my office. A few minutes before the end of the school day, I would go to the mothers' waiting room, where Brian and I would meet to go home.

Jane left it to me to schedule an appointment with her if I wanted one. Occasionally, I called to fill her in on Brian and to catch up on news in general. In fact, we kept in touch even after Brian was no longer at Wilder.

During the first four years of Brian's life, I took lots of pictures of the children, but I never had time to sort them out and put them into the baby books I had for each child. One raw and rainy night, my husband away on a business trip and the children all in bed, I fixed myself a dish of coffee fudge ice cream and took it into the living room, where I had built a fire. I sat in front of the fire, eating my ice cream, with the children's pictures spread all around me. Suddenly I found I didn't want to face this compilation of photographs that showed Brian in a rage or running into something. One by one, I began to feed them into the fire. I destroyed the originals and the negatives, until all that remained were pictures in which Brian looked happy and angelic.

I divided the pictures into four groups so that each book would have mostly pictures of one particular child but would include some photos of the other three. It grew late, and the fire burned down to hot ash. I placed each child's stack of pictures in his or her baby book and went to bed. Gluing would have to wait until another free night.

❖   ❖   ❖

It was during the group session in March, a month before Brian's fifth birthday, that Dr. Sims, Brian's psychologist, said the words that still haunt me: "Brian will never be normal, Mrs. Hart. I earnestly suggest that you consider institutionalizing him and concentrate your efforts on your other three children who, unlike Brian, can learn."

"No" was all I could say. I sat there utterly stunned, thoughts whirling through my head. If Brian's doctor had such a negative attitude about his future, how could she possibly help him? What did she mean, he couldn't learn? What about all the things I had already taught him? No, he couldn't draw a picture of a boat with people in it. But he could make one out of clay. He had brought home from school a wonderful boat with three people in it that he had made from clay. How could you say a child couldn't learn, when he was shrewd enough to refuse to do something on the grounds that a machine couldn't hear him do it? To help him practice his speech, I had gotten Brian a tape that came with a workbook. The tape player would say the name of the picture in the workbook and then say, "Now you say 'apple'." Brian had tried the first few and then had flatly refused to respond. When I asked why, he had looked up at me and said, "The machine can't hear me."

Dr. Sims's statement haunted me for weeks. I fought to eradicate those words from my mind, but I knew I was losing the battle. Any peace found at home deteriorated as other problems multiplied and my worry increased. "What should I do?" The question circled frantically in my mind. Finally, things seemed so out of hand that I didn't see how I was going to stabilize any of our lives again, let alone raise Brian. Kelly, who was fighting her own battles with learning disabilities, slammed doors and ran through the house hysterically; Whitney retreated to her room, read continuously, and had frequent headaches; Penny did puzzles alone and withdrew more and more into herself. Brian became increasingly disruptive and destructive, lashing out at everyone and everything, hitting his sisters and throwing food at meals.

It seemed that every time I put out a fire, two more erupted. School and tutors for Kelly were leaving her frustrated and angry, but every day I had to plan the steps needed for

Brian to grasp a new skill. How could I tutor Kelly? I was swimming harder and harder, but I felt myself sinking deeper and deeper. I tried talking to Jay, but he didn't seem to understand my concerns. Eventually, my tears became ungovernable. For three days I cried almost continuously while doing all the things I had to do. Sleep became impossible.

Things came to a head one Sunday morning. When Jay woke that morning, I told him I didn't know how I was going to get through the day and that I needed his help to do so. I asked him to get the children dressed and give them breakfast. I had promised a friend, who was out of town, that I would take her children for the day. I asked Jay to make a plan for all of us and told him I'd do whatever he planned, the zoo, some kind of outing, or whatever. As Jay dressed, I fell asleep. The next thing I knew, the children were climbing on my bed, still in their pajamas. They had not had breakfast and told me, "Dad's gone to play tennis at Uncle Roy's." I called my brother-in-law and told him what was going on and that Jay had to come home. Jay returned but phoned my parents in Chicago. When I refused to speak to them, they said they would come immediately. I don't recall what we did that Sunday, but I do remember my parents arrived in the late afternoon.

That evening, after we had put the children to bed, my father suggested the four of us go into the living room to talk. He asked how they could help and what we saw as the major problem. Jay said nothing. I just said that I didn't know what to do about Brian, that I wasn't going to put him in an institution. My parents and I discussed the situation at length. Each time we brought up a possible option, Jay was against it: no to boarding school; no to a person coming to live in our home to teach Brian and care for him; no to starting our own school; and on and on. Finally, my mother said, "Jay, what do you want?" meaning, What do you want to be done about Brian? Jay said, "I want out," left the room, and went to bed.

Fighting back the tears, I turned to my parents and begged, "I need help. Please don't leave Boston until I have some direction for Brian." My father replied quietly, "Mom will stay as long as needed, and I will return on weekends if necessary. That's enough for one night. Get some sleep. We'll talk again in the morning."

After nearly a week of examining alternatives, I finally decided to keep Brian in Wilder. I had wanted to withdraw him immediately, but with only a few weeks left in the school year and no tolerable alternative, I decided to stick with what we had and braced myself to continue.

That summer Brian attended Green Acres Day Camp. By chance, a Harvard lecturer and researcher named Marshall Haith was working with the campers there. As part of his research, Haith would have the children look through a viewer as he flashed symbols at them. Most of the children could identify the symbols even when they were presented for as little as one tenth of a second. Brian could not, Haith told Mrs. Mitchell, but he noticed that when Brian had a full second he could identify them. Haith wondered if Brian had demonstrated other indications of perceptual irregularities. (In the 1960s learning problems were frequently attributed to flaws in sensory perception. Our knowledge of how the brain works is much more sophisticated now than it was thirty years ago. Most researchers and clinicians today believe that the major cause of learning problems lies not in receiving information, but in processing it in the brain.)

Mrs. Mitchell shared Marshall Haith's comments with me. I wasn't sure what they meant for Brian, but it was better than the stony silence I faced at Wilder. At Mrs. Mitchell's urging, I took Brian to Massachusetts General Hospital for new neurological testing. Dr. Scholl, the neurologist, found that Brian had some visual/motor/perceptual difficulty. In very simple terms, this seemed to mean Brian had some trouble with eye-hand coordination. She also noted he had trouble with abstract thinking and would probably have trouble with arithmetic. She recommended a transitional class—something between kindergarten and first grade—for next fall. It was this comment that brightened my life. Here was a doctor who believed Brian could learn. All I needed for next year was a transitional class.

In the middle of August, Cristina arrived from Spain to visit. She spent time with Brian and observed him at day camp. "Brian can be normal someday," she assured me. "I've seen other children like this, and some, with dedicated mothers, have turned out well. Try to keep him with normal kids," she told me.

Although Cristina's support and optimism further lightened my outlook, I still had days when I wondered how Brian was ever going to cope in the world outside his home. He still continued to confuse various words, such as *sheets* with *sheep's* and *shoes* with *Sue's*. Sometimes he understood the words if he could get the correct meaning from the rest of the sentence, but if I simply said, "Bring me the sheets," rather than "Bring me the sheets that are in the clothes dryer," he might appear with sheep from his toy farm set. Although the hearing test indicated that his hearing was fine, I wondered if sometimes the sounds came through to him in some sort of jumble. And no matter how optimistic Cristina might feel, his behavior was still a problem.

For example, on the hottest day of the summer, Jay, the four children, and I piled into our station wagon and drove to Cape Cod to spend the day on the beach with friends and their children. En route, Brian removed his shoes and socks and threw them out the partially opened rear window. After retrieving them, we arrived at the beach and spread blankets out on the sand. Once Brian was happily engrossed in building a sand castle, we left him with his father and one other father and went for a walk on the beach. Between our blankets and the water sat a mother and daughter oiling themselves. While we were gone, Brian picked up his bucket, went to the water, and filled it. It was when Brian approached the perspiring women, who were now lying with their eyes closed, soaking in the sun, that Jay realized what he was about to do, but it was too late. Brian dumped the bucket of water over the woman's head. "But, lady hot," Brian responded when he was scolded. If he had been two or three, I thought at the time, it would have been a funny story. But he was five, and it was no longer funny.

I could not think of an alternative to Wilder for Brian, but at the same time, I couldn't see that he was getting anything from it. In September 1967, with grave misgivings on my part, Brian and I returned to Wilder two mornings a week.

Worry about Brian's development made me more short-tempered than ever, which was hard on Kelly, Whitney, and Penny. It also left me unobservant. I had not paid particular attention to Kelly's struggles in school, and I did not notice that I was always saying to her, "Sit still. Pay attention."

7

Saying No to an Expert

"Dr. Sims says the reason I'm always getting hurt is that I'm trying to kill myself."

—Brian, age five

The very first week he was back at Wilder, Brian began to regress. He was more moody than he had been and more prone to throwing himself on the floor, hitting, kicking, and screaming. He seemed to be permanently angry. Hoping to cheer him up, I took him and baby-sitter Barbara with me for a quick trip out to visit my parents. They met us at the arrival gate at O'Hare, and we walked to the baggage claim area together. While we were waiting for our suitcases, Brian announced to me, "I've seen them [meaning his grandparents]. I want to go home now."

I was dumbfounded, and my father intervened. "Brian," he said, "you are going to spend a few days in my house, and in my house I have the final say."

Brian said, "But you go to work."

"Yes, Brian, I go to work, and when I'm gone, Mama has the final say. When Mama isn't home, your mom has the final say, and when your mom is out, Barbara has the final say. You are never in charge in my house."

Brian spent the first part of our visit with a frown on his face. Then one day my father picked him up and stood him on the sink in the bathroom facing the mirror. Dad put a big smile on his face and put his head next to Brian's so Brian could see his own face and his grandfather's at the same time. Brian looked at Papa's big grin and his own frown and began to smile. Papa told him that everyone looks better when they smile. Brian seemed to cheer up and behaved for the rest of the visit.

Shortly after our return, Barbara awoke to a terrible smell. Her room was separated from the kitchen by a short hall where Chips, our dog, was tied up at night. When Barbara entered the hall, she found Chips surrounded by mounds of food that had made him violently ill. He was floundering in vomit and diarrhea. She put the poor dog out, cleaned up the mess, then showered and dressed. Then she entered the kitchen/breakfast room. The table, which was always set the night before, was covered with food and beverages that Brian and Penny had taken from the cabinets and refrigerator. All the glasses on the table had been filled to overflowing with orange juice, Coke, and milk. Liquids stood in pools on the table and dripped off the edges onto the chairs and floor. Sugar, flour, coffee, cereal, noodles, rice, crackers, and cookies combined with the liquids, carpeting the kitchen and breakfast room floors.

It was more than Barbara could cope with. She walked into my room in tears and announced that she was leaving.

When I saw the mess and heard what she had already cleaned up, I gave her the day off, and I sent Brian and Penny to their rooms, telling them they were not to come out until I said so. Kelly and Whitney ate breakfast in the dining room, and after sending them off to school, I cleaned up the mess. I knew the activity had been Brian's inspiration and that Penny had simply followed his orders.

At Green Acres Brian's behavior became so disruptive that Mrs. Mitchell told me that he could remain in kindergarten only if a teacher's aide was added to his class. To keep Brian there, I agreed to pay for the teaching assistant. At the same time, Mrs. Mitchell asked if I would be interested in having Rosalie Richardson, a consultant and trustee of Green Acres as well as a teacher of brain-damaged children in another town's school system, look at Brian. I immediately agreed and a month later, Rosalie came to observe Brian and speak with me.

At the time of her visit, Brian was fascinated with blocks and spent many hours building. When he and I constructed things together at home, there was never a problem, but the structures Brian built alone always collapsed, and he would become furious, kicking and throwing the blocks everywhere. As a result, an adult had to be in the playroom at home at all times to protect Brian and his sisters, because two of the playroom's walls were windows.

Watching Brian with his blocks, Rosalie noticed that he started his buildings with two unequal blocks. "The next time Brian begins building, take his first two blocks and bang them together," she said. "Then stand them upright on the floor, put Brian's hand on top of the two blocks, and say: These blocks are not the same size. When you build you must always start with two blocks that are the same."

From the moment I carried out Rosalie's directions, Brian's buildings no longer fell, and the building-block temper tantrums ceased.

Even then, however, Brian seemed almost out of control. He would run through the dining room knocking over the chairs, one after another. His frustration with everything seemed overwhelming. Then, at the end of one morning in early December, he burst into the mothers' waiting room sobbing hysterically.

"Brian, what happened? What's the matter?" I asked as I pulled him into my arms.

He continued to cry, gasping for air. Finally he sniffled and as he exhaled said, "Dr. Sims says—" He took in more air and let it out, "the reason I'm always getting hurt—" his lips quivered and tears ran down his cheeks, "is that I'm trying to kill myself."

I held him close to me, feeling his chest pound against mine. I couldn't believe that anyone would say such a thing to a five-year-old.

"Brian," I asked incredulously, "did Dr. Sims really tell you the reason you've gotten hurt so much is that you're trying to kill yourself?" I had good reason to know it wasn't true. I had mopped up his tears and held his shaking body often enough when he had put his hand through a window or rammed painfully into some object.

He nodded his head up and down on my shoulder.

Suddenly the dam broke. I picked him up and ran down the dark, narrow hall, his head and arms bouncing on my shoulder. He was heavy and I switched him to my side so some of his weight was supported by my hip as I climbed the stairs. Still, I was panting by the time I reached Dr. Sims's office. The door was ajar. I gave it a hard push with my right hand, and it banged against the wall as I entered.

"Did you really tell Brian he's trying to kill himself?" I demanded.

Dr. Sims rose from behind her desk. She glared at me furiously. "Mrs. Hart," she said, "you're out of line barging in here like this, first of all, and, second, this is exactly how I feel about Brian. Obviously his behavior is. . . ."

"You're the one who's out of line," I shouted before she could finish her sentence. And with that I whirled around and slammed the office door behind me. As I hauled Brian down the stairs, I looked around and realized with utter relief that we would never again set foot in this building.

I reached our car and put Brian down to find the keys at the bottom of my purse. My hand shook so badly as I put the key in the lock that I had to steady it with my other hand. Brian climbed in and I moved to the center of the seat, away from the steering wheel, and pulled him onto my lap. As I held him in my arms, I struggled to bring myself under control.

"Dr. Sims is wrong," I said to him. "I know that you're not trying to kill yourself." He tightened his grip on me as I talked. We stayed in each other's arms for several minutes.

"Brian," I continued, taking his arms from around my neck and looking into his face, "we'll find a better way. Don't you doubt it."

That night, I felt cowardly and brave at the same time. Leaving Wilder with Brian the way I had scared me. I had told an expert she was wrong and had withdrawn my child from school. Yet, I really felt I was doing the right thing. But how was I going to cope with Brian and give my girls their fair share of my time? As I lay in bed unable to sleep, I made up my mind that I would simply have to be more efficient in everything. Now I would need all the energy I could find, which had to start with getting enough sleep. I willed myself to sleep.

The following day, as I did my usual errands and car pools, I decided to keep Brian at Green Acres full time until the end of the academic year. I knew this wouldn't prepare him for first grade the following September, but at least Brian would be exposed to the preparation and be with normal children.

One Thursday morning in February, when the children had finished breakfast and left the table, I sat staring at my untouched breakfast, wondering what to do next. My mother, who had been spending a week with me once a month since the previous spring, sipped her coffee slowly.

"The baby-sitter will be here today," she said, "and she'll be watching Brian. Why don't we take the day off? We'll do anything you like. Do you want to go shopping and out to lunch?"

"I'm sorry, Mom," I said, lowering my head. "I have no idea. I don't care if I eat and I have no interest in buying anything. I just want answers for Brian. That's all that matters to me."

As I finished speaking, Rosalie Richardson called. "I'm driving to New Hampshire this evening, and I thought you might like to come along," she said. "I'll be spending the day at Crotched Mountain School tomorrow, and I think you'd find it an interesting place to visit. The school's diagnostician, Diane, is a friend of mine, and we can spend tonight at her house." It was the first thing that had sounded appealing to me in weeks, and I told her I would go. Mother was delighted to see my spirits rise.

Rosalie picked me up late that afternoon. We had dinner en route and arrived at Diane's shortly after 10:00 P.M. It wasn't until we pulled into the driveway that Rosalie announced, "I hope you like cats. Diane has at least twenty of them." I happen to be allergic to cats, and twenty sounded like quite a few. Realizing there was no easy way out of the situation, I braced myself and said nothing beyond "wow." It's probably best that I didn't know what that night would be like. A film of cat hair covered the furniture, counter tops, and floors in every room, including the one bathroom that housed a cat-litter box. On the kitchen floor were ten bowls holding varying amounts of water or cat food, surrounded by spillover. The smell of fish and cats permeated everything.

Rosalie, Diane, and I had a cup of tea together, then I said I was tired and wanted to go to bed. I planned to shut my bedroom door, open the window wide, and breathe deeply. Diane, a warm, friendly woman, showed me my bedroom and said to give a call if I needed anything. It was then that I discovered the door from my bedroom to the hall was missing and that someone had painted the window shut so there was no hope of opening it. That night there was a constant parade of cats through my room, several stopping for an hour or more to sleep on my bed. By morning my nose ran, my eyes itched, and sleep was only something I had heard about in the past.

Our visit to Crotched Mountain School, however, made up for my itching eyes and runny nose. The morning class I audited contained five learning-disabled children, ranging from six to eight years old. The teacher was covering the names of the days of the week, and she asked the children to talk about their favorite days. Susie went first. Friday was her favorite day.

"Tell us why," the teacher said.

"Because it jumps," answered Susie.

Neither her teacher nor I understood what Susie meant, but the teacher persevered.

"What do you do on Friday, Susie?" she asked.

"I go home on Friday," answered Susie.

"And when you get home, what happens?"

"I open the door, and Rusty, my dog, jumps on me."

"I understand," said the teacher. "Susie likes Friday best because she goes home and is with her dog." Susie beamed and the other children nodded.

After class, I asked the teacher what was wrong with Susie that made her respond, "Friday jumps." Brian, too, exhibited this type of speech. The teacher said she didn't know the cause, but the condition was known as fragmentary speech. Finally, I had a name for Brian's speech.

8

Learning Is Possible

I found myself wondering if we should teach Brian cursive writing rather than printing.

—Nancy

I came home from Crotched Mountain School filled with hope and new ideas for Brian. I had seen an assortment of seriously handicapped children with a variety of learning problems, yet all of those children were learning. During the drive up and back, Rosalie and I had discussed Brian's problems in depth. Rosalie, too, had had insights and ideas based on her experiences in the classroom.

For the rest of the year, Brian continued to wreak a fair amount of havoc at Green Acres. Still, he seemed calmer, I thought. Green Acres offered him a certain structure for his day times, and as chaotic as our home might seem at times, it was home and provided security. True, he didn't slow down any. There were still outbursts of rage when he didn't understand something or when he tried to do something and it didn't come out as it should, but now the creativity that underlay some of his doings was more apparent.

One day I went to do some errands and left Barbara with the children. I was gone over two hours, and I was afraid Barbara would be overwhelmed. As I rushed up the back steps with the groceries, Brian, all smiles, grabbed me and pulled me into the basement. "Come see my raft."

He had nailed together nearly every board in the basement, sawed off the handle of our broom, and installed it as the mast. On the mast hung part of one of my best sheets. To haul it up and down, he had used a section of our clothes line.

I was speechless for several minutes but finally managed to inquire if the sheet had come from the linen closet. He smiled brilliantly and said, "Yes. I wanted to use the things on my window with the strings already in them. But you wouldn't like that," which utterly disarmed me. I found with Brian I often vacillated between a guilty wanting to get rid of him and a respectful awe for his enormous enterprise and creativity. If I could just find the right school or the right teacher, I thought, he would have a chance to be a happy, productive adult.

The girls, of course, were amazed when I did not punish him for destroying the sheet, broom, and clothes line. Kelly, in particular, was furious. She knew she would have been punished if she had done what Brian had. I reverted to my old line, "He's a boy, and boys do things like this until they grow up and know better." I doubt any of the girls liked the double standard, but I didn't know how else to handle the situation. I couldn't punish Brian every time he did something wrong. As it was, he was sent to his room or lost privileges far more often than the girls. I reserved punishment for Brian for his most serious, possibly life-threatening offenses.

These offenses were slightly less frequent now because it was gradually becoming easier to communicate with Brian and because of two invaluable assistants: Tony Parnofiello, an undergraduate at Boston College who had watched over Brian the year before, and Gertrude Peterson, a longtime, once-a-week employee and treasured family friend who was still watching over Brian.

Tony was a warm, energetic, and altogether remarkable young man, already interested in becoming a pediatrician. He had spent several afternoons a week with Brian, just being his friend and companion, from the time Brian was four and a half until the summer after his fifth birthday. Tony had a real knack for side-tracking Brian's explosions and for saving him from situations in which he might feel like he had failed, like Pee Wee League baseball.

In the spring of 1967, we had signed Brian up for Pee Wee League, thinking it would be good for him to be around other boys his age, doing what they did. After all, how serious could you be about baseball played by five-year-olds? Shortly before 6:00 P.M. on the afternoon of the first practice, Tony had taken Brian to the park. They had set off as the rest of us sat down to dinner, and to my surprise, they were back before we had finished dessert. Before I could inquire how practice had gone, Tony had put his finger to his lips, swung Brian off his shoulders, and had marched him to the kitchen sink so he could wash his hands before eating.

Later, while Brian was in his room getting ready for bed, Tony joined me in the kitchen and gave me a rundown of the practice. The coach, he said, was only interested in boys who knew how to play baseball and were good at it. Brian's baseball skills were not developed, although he certainly could run fast enough, and he didn't know the rules or understand the lingo, all of which could trigger a major explosion as Brian's frustration grew, Tony pointed out.

When they had arrived at the park, the coach had put Brian in right field. Fortunately, since he was watching planes flying overhead most of the time like many other five-year-olds, no balls were hit to him. Eventually Brian's team came up to bat. Several youngsters batted, and then the coach had yelled, "Hey, Hart, you're up next." Tony said Brian looked up at him questioningly. He handed Brian a bat, pointed to home plate, and patted him on the shoulder. Brian went to the plate and never took the bat off his shoulders as the pitcher threw four straight balls. "You got a walk, kid—take it!" the coach yelled. When Brian started to walk off the field, the coach grabbed the bat from him and yelled, "Take first!"

Tony said, "I pointed to the bag and Brian went over and stood on it. The next boy hit an infield fly to the second baseman, and the coach yelled at Brian, 'Hold first.' Brian bent over and tried to pick up the bag he was standing on. The first baseman told Brian to stand up and leave the bag alone. The next kid who came up to bat hit a ground ball single between first and second bases. The coach yelled at Brian to take second, and I pointed to the bag, but by the time Brian understood what he was to do, he was tagged out and the coach was furious." Tony stopped for a moment and then said, "I decided it was time for dinner. Perhaps Brian and I should play a little baseball together and try Pee Wee League next year."

All I could do was to think, "Thank you, heaven, for Tony and his intuitive understanding of Brian." Tony helped with Brian for that year, then he went on to other work. His work with Brian, however, had been an important influence along Brian's developmental path.

Gertrude Peterson, whom the children still call "Peanut," had started working for me when Kelly was nine months old. Peanut was a warm, loving woman with a good sense of humor, which she needed at our house. She had been born in Poland but had grown up and married in Germany. Her husband was reported missing two weeks before the end of World War II and a few weeks before the birth of their son. Still nursing her baby, Peanut fled from the advancing Soviet army. In the years immediately following the war, she struggled to support herself and raise her son. Although she prayed for news of her husband, none ever came, and eventually he was listed as killed in action.

When Peanut's son died as a result of peritonitis after a burst appendix, she suffered a breakdown. On the advice of a friend, she emigrated to Boston, where she married a German widower with two young daughters. She had been in the United States only a few months when she answered my newspaper ad and thus joined our family.

Although she did not know how to teach Brian and she, like the rest of us, did not understand what was causing his behavior, Peanut could always handle him. If Brian got out of hand, she simply took off her slipper and held it up for Brian to see. He got the message and did what Peanut wanted, yet she never touched him in anger. Peanut was a second mother to the children and a confidante and friend to me. Without her, I doubt I would have been able to maintain my equilibrium during Brian's early years. Peanut's efforts gave me the time I needed to visit schools and learn, from anyone who was willing to share time with me, more about how to handle Brian.

Rosalie and I, for example, met frequently to talk after our trip to Crotched Mountain. While Green Acres worked to expose Brian to the information he needed to be prepared for first grade, whenever that might happen, I worked to reinforce it. Now to the daily tutoring sessions that Brian and I had begun when he was at the Wilder Center, I added numbers and letters made from wood, felt, and sandpaper; finger paints; crayons; and other concrete materials. I invented activities in which he used his fingers and was rewarded, usually with a pretzel, for correct responses. Both unconsciously and consciously through Rosalie, Crotched Mountain, and visits to other schools, I came to realize that the sense of touch for young children is often, although not in every case, the most important sense. When there is either a visual or an auditory perception or acuity problem, it is even more important. Although no one was yet sure where Brian's problems lay, this seemed to be the easiest way for him to learn.

I didn't want to overwhelm Brian with tutoring sessions, but I did hope to find someone who could give him one more hour in the day than I had. Neither Rosalie nor I, however, were able to find an appropriate tutor for him. It was at this point that I went to visit Cove School in Evanston, Illinois.

I had heard of Cove School through my father. As I searched through New England for help for Brian, my parents combed the Midwest. After reading an article that described the behavior of some children who were classified as perceptually handicapped, my father had joined the Fund for the Perceptually Handicapped in Evanston. The label did not interest him, but the description of some of the behavior had made him think of Brian. After joining the organization, he began to send me their literature, which I eagerly read. He also met Dr. Laura Lehtinen Rogan, the co-founder of Cove School and the co-author of *Psychopathology and Education of the Brain Injured Child*, which was the first authoritative book on learning disabilities. Dr. Rogan was also a collaborator on *The Other Child*, the first book for parents of children with learning disabilities.

At my father's suggestion, I called Dr. Rogan and arranged to spend a day at the school with her. Like my experience at Crotched Mountain School, my visit to Cove School was a real eye opener.

The classes were small, and the classrooms were stripped of the decorations usually found in classrooms. Sights and sounds that could distract the children from what they were doing were kept to a minimum. Although many of the students were hyperactive, they were all in control of themselves and constructively busy.

In one class, I saw children using different cardboard forms in math to help them do their calculations. (Later, I duplicated these forms, first in wood and then in cardboard, for Brian.) In another class, children practiced cursive writing on specially lined paper, using only the lower-case letters that did not extend above or below the lines (*a, c, e, i, m, n, o, r, s, u, v, w, x*). Another specially lined paper was used by children practicing lower-case letters with stems extending above the line (*b, d, h, k, l, t*), and a third specially lined paper was used by those learning to write the lower-case letters that went below the line (*f, g, j, p, q, y, z*). Capital letters were taught and practiced on still another specially lined paper.

The paper fascinated me. Brian had to fight just to get an X somewhere on a piece of paper, and even then you couldn't be sure it was an X. It frustrated him immensely because he always knew it wasn't right. Dr. Rogan explained, "All children at Cove School are taught cursive writing. Since all letters in a word are attached, this facilitates a child's knowing where one word ends and the next begins, and it decreases the number of times a child has to stop and lift his pencil." I found myself wondering if we should plan to teach Brian cursive writing rather than printing.

Perhaps it was that thought when I returned home that pushed me into my next step. With less than three weeks of Green Acres kindergarten remaining, I had begun to wonder before my trip what I would do with Brian during the days, even with our daily tutoring sessions. Brian's curiosity never ended and could lead to disasters.

After much discussion with Rosalie, I decided to transfer Brian to Rosalie's educable retarded class, which still had two months to run before summer break. I felt the structured learning situation and individualized attention Rosalie could provide would help Brian pick up some more of the skills he needed. But to get him into Rosalie's class, I needed a physician's diagnosis. By now, Brian had been given many labels— "exceptional child," "emotionally disturbed," "hyperactive"—but no single label, and none of these labels accurately described my son. The only way I could get him into Rosalie's class was to sign a form stating that he was brain-damaged and mentally retarded. Both Rosalie and I felt that it was far more important for Brian to receive the education he needed then than to worry about what people would think about the diagnosis or his attendance in her class. Rosalie assured me that the paper would be destroyed the day he came out of her class, and she kept her word.

9

Beginning to Get Some Answers

"I'm tired in here. She makes me think."

—Brian, pointing to his head

About the time Brian entered Rosalie's class, I changed pediatricians. During a visit to my parents, I had met a friend of theirs who was a pediatrician. Because my father had already intrigued him with a description of Brian, I had no qualms about asking him what he thought could be done. He said that while it was undoubtedly true that boys could be very active, there were some drugs that could help control hyperactivity. He recommended that when we got back to Boston we should arrange to see Dr. William Berenberg, who was at Children's Hospital. I promptly called Dr. Berenberg when I got home and made an appointment for Brian and me. Dr. Berenberg admitted that he did not know what was wrong with Brian nor how it might best be treated, but he was willing to try medication to control Brian's hyperactivity. He said that the best he could do was support me in my dealings with the schools. He related well to Brian, and I liked his honesty and trusted him.

We began to experiment with medications. I wanted Brian on Ritalin, which my parents' friend had mentioned as a possibility, but Dr. Berenberg wanted to try Dexedrine, an amphetamine, first. (Amphetamines can have the paradoxical effect of calming typically hyperactive children.) Although I was fairly numb to most forms of chaos by the time we switched to Dr. Berenberg, I do know the day Brian took his first dose of the drug was one of the worst days of my life. Brian's normal hyperactivity was scarcely manageable; with the Dexedrine, he looked like a film run on fast forward. I was afraid to leave him alone in his room. At midnight, when he was still jumping and turning somersaults on our bed, I decided to give him a sleeping pill. Fortunately, Jay was so tired that he simply stated I was making a big mistake in giving a sleeping pill to a child. He went to sleep as I grabbed Brian and carried him into the bathroom.

I emptied half the capsule into the toilet and the other half into a spoon. After adding orange juice to the spoon, I said, "Brian, swallow this. It will help you go to sleep." Within half an hour, Brian was asleep, and that horrendous day was over.

Next, Dilantin, a drug used to control epilepsy, was tried. Brian had had at least one episode that might have been a seizure. We didn't know. Brian and I had been alone in the house one day during one of our tutoring sessions. There had been no music on, no distractions whatsoever, and we had been working quite peacefully when all of a sudden Brian began to scream. He screamed and threw himself around and threw around anything within reach for at least a full minute. Then he abruptly stopped. It scared me to death, but we never found out what caused it. Dilantin, however, had no effect.

Finally, Dr. Berenberg put Brian on Ritalin. When I tucked Brian in bed at the end of his first day on Ritalin, he said: "Mom, you know I have a motor in me that all the time goes *bzzzzz*. But with these pills it goes *bum, bum, bum*."

Brian's transfer to Rosalie's class was made at the end of April, a few days after his sixth birthday, and coincided with his beginning to take Ritalin. The combination of Ritalin and Rosalie was phenomenal. Ritalin decreased Brian's hyperactivity and increased his ability to concentrate. Rosalie provided a challenging, structured environment in which Brian's energies were productively channeled. At the end of each day, he was mentally and physically exhausted. He was also relaxed, calm, and happy. When I picked him up at the end of his first day, he sauntered to the car and collapsed on the front seat.

"What's wrong?" I asked, shocked by this unprecedented behavior.

Brian pointed to his head. "I'm tired in here," he said "She makes me think!"

His class consisted of six children: two with Down syndrome, three with other organic problems and some mental deficiency, and another boy named Brian, who had been institutionalized at birth. (After Rosalie's efforts, this child scored normally on an IQ test, was discharged from the institution, and was put up for adoption.) The children were a year or two older than Brian, yet neither taller nor stronger. Intellectually, Brian was close to the developmental level of the two most advanced boys.

Shortly before Father's Day, Rosalie called to tell me about Brian's conversation with the other Brian in her class. During project time, when all the youngsters were making Father's Day gifts, the other Brian had said he didn't know to whom he could give his gift. Brian said, "Give it to your father."

"I don't have a father," responded the other Brian.

"Then give it to your mother," Brian said.

"I don't have a mother either," said the other Brian.

Looking very sad, Brian said, "Oh, I'm sorry. Then you really are poor."

As Rosalie repeated this conversation, I found myself thinking we were finally on our way to the kind of life I knew Brian could have. Still, even as I watched Brian begin to bloom under Rosalie's carefully structured program, I realized we had just begun the battle. Rosalie would not always be there to feed him directions step by step. Sooner or later, he would have to be able to follow a series of directions. That night I told Brian to go to the bathroom, brush his teeth, go to the toilet, put his slippers in his closet, and wait for me on his bed. Then I willed myself to stay seated in the family room as he ran off. After a few minutes, I went to his room. I found him sitting on his bed with his slippers on. He had not entered the bathroom.

Over the next week or so, I tried giving Brian one or two directions at night. I found that if I asked him *either* to brush his teeth *or* to go to the toilet *or* to put his slippers in his closet *or* to wait for me on his bed, he could do it. But if I combined any two of the activities—"brush your teeth and go to the toilet"—he did only the last activity I mentioned.

Finally one night, I called Dr. Rogan at home and explained the situation. "What should I do?" I asked.

"You are probably overloading Brian with too many words," Dr. Rogan replied. "Use only concrete, visual ones. Tell him: *teeth, toilet, slippers, bed.* Then send him off."

What a miracle those words of wisdom created! The next night I followed Dr. Rogan's directions, and Brian did it all.

Indeed, that spring, when Brian joined Rosalie's class, acted as a harbinger of answers to many of the questions I had had about Brian, although at the time I didn't recognize it. At that moment I was wondering what to do with Brian when Rosalie's class ended, which it would do very shortly. Where was the right school and the right class for Brian? I wasn't sure repeating kindergarten would help Brian move forward, even with Rosalie's teaching. Dr. Scholl had recommended a transitional class and, after my visits to Crotched Mountain School and Cove School, I knew the type of classroom situation that would be best for him. Unfortunately, I could find nothing like this in the greater Boston area.

In desperation I began to interview all the first grade teachers in the Brookline public school system. The teacher I liked best taught at the Heath School, the closest school to our home, so I enrolled Brian in Heath for the fall, although realistically I wondered how he was going to cope. Besides the learning disability that we knew of and the hyperactivity, which Ritalin was handling, Brian was still constantly running into furniture and other things.

Doctors at two Boston hospitals had checked Brian's eyes and assured me that there was nothing wrong with his vision. I had almost stopped wondering about it until I heard, at a NACLD (National Association of Children with Learning Disabilities) conference in Boston, an impressive lecture by Dr. Abe Kirshner, an eye doctor who ran a clinic in Montreal for children with perceptual problems similar to Brian's. After months of phoning Dr. Kirshner daily, I finally reached him directly. Frustrated by the delay, I announced abruptly: "I want to bring my son to Montreal today. Please agree to see him this afternoon."

After a brief conversation, Dr. Kirshner asked if I knew a Dr. McDonald, in Newton, Massachusetts, who did work very similar to his own. I said I didn't, and Dr. Kirshner offered to make an appointment for Brian to be seen by Dr. McDonald that very day. He also promised to see Brian himself in Montreal if I wasn't satisfied with Dr. McDonald's diagnosis and recommendations.

That same day, Brian and I went to Dr. McDonald's Newton office. Dr. McDonald did not ask me a single question before telling Brian to climb into his chair. After examining Brian's eyes for about two minutes, he turned to me and asked, "Is your son constantly getting injured?" I was so shocked that all I could do was nod affirmatively.

"Your son has no working peripheral vision," he said. So, I thought, perhaps that was why Brian could sleep with his eyes partly open.

Taking Brian out of the examining chair and standing him in the doorway to another room, Dr. McDonald explained, "Brian, most people have two kinds of seeing, but you have only one. Therefore, before you enter a room or move at all, you must move your head or your eyes to see where things are. If you can remember to do this, you will not get hurt any more often than other little boys."

Dr. McDonald moved Brian's head to the right and then to the left to demonstrate to Brian what he needed to do. Then he outlined exercises that I could try with Brian and told me honestly that he did not know if they would help. We agreed that Brian would attend one of Dr. McDonald's classes twice a week.

That night, when Brian went to bed, he was very quiet. He lay on his back—no cars, no engine noise, no imaginary road races. "What's wrong?" I asked. "Do you feel all right?"

He gazed up at me with the angry bewilderment that one only sees in the very young or the very old. "Mommy, why didn't you make me right, and when are you going to get my eyes fixed so they will work like other people's?"

I sat down on the bed and put him in my lap, his fists still clenched. I hugged him and said, "Neither the doctors nor I know how to fix them. But if you use your eyes the way Dr. McDonald told you to, you will be fine."

I was relieved to have an answer by then, but the hurt inside me for Brian was terrible. Six years of coping with a problem nobody recognized seemed like an awful lot for a little boy.

My next source of answers came in the shape of Vera Moretti. Over the summer, Rosalie had been continuing the search for a tutor. One evening at the end of August, she called to say she had found just the right person for Brian and also for Kelly, who had struggled through fourth grade growing more unhappy by the day. The tutor's name, Rosalie said, was Vera Moretti. One meeting convinced me that Vera was the right person. I was fascinated by the background of this bright, energetic, sensitive, creative woman who had such a genuine interest in problem children.

She was the daughter of two child-prodigies. Her father, a Russian Jew, was a concert violinist. Her mother, who was Greek Orthodox, was a concert pianist. With Vera's uncle, an outstanding cellist, the three had toured Europe as "The Russian Trio." As a young woman, Vera had studied music in Germany, but with Hitler's rise to power she had had to flee from Germany to Austria. By the time the Germans entered Austria, Vera had reestablished herself as one of the leading actresses in Vienna. With the Nazi invasion came renewed restrictions and threats to her life. Eventually, Paramount Pictures managed to get her from Vienna to Paris on an overnight pass, and once in Paris, she fled to the United States.

Vera arrived in New York with the clothes on her back and very little money. Paramount initially gave her a place to stay but couldn't use her in movies because she didn't speak English. They did, however, give her a desk job, and she learned to say, "The boss is out" and "The boss is in a meeting." In time, Vera learned English mostly through movies and TV, got a job as a night club singer, and eventually became the lead performer at the Reuban Bleu in New York City. Throughout it all, she saved whatever money she could in order to bring her husband to the States, which she finally did.

Shortly after the birth of their second child, Vera's husband died, leaving her with two infant sons to support. Because all her papers had been destroyed during the war, including her certificates from the conservatory in Berlin, she had to teach at private boarding schools rather than universities. The schools gave her a salary, a place for the family to live, and eventually an education for her boys.

At the time of our meeting, Vera was using music therapy with blind, hearing impaired, deaf, retarded, and physically handicapped patients in the Green Blind Unit of the Fernald State School for the Retarded. She invited me to observe her afternoon class. Although she had described her class, I was stunned by what I saw. I had never seen such a group of damaged persons. In the middle of them stood Vera, a totally caring teacher. Through her extraordinary singing and composing talents, combined with her exceptional ability to understand the different ways each of these individuals learned, she brought harmony, joy, self-esteem, and hope to the class. In the months ahead, I would frequently observe Vera's classes, and I never ceased to be amazed by the slow but steady progress her students made.

The following week, which was the beginning of September 1968, Vera began tutoring Kelly and Brian in the late afternoon. From time to time, she would stay for dinner, which gave her more time to work with Brian and allowed Kelly to participate in after-school sports. One late-September evening after tutoring, Vera, who knew Brian had been seen by many doctors, came to me and said, "I know what you think of the experts, but I think you ought to have Kelly and Brian tested by Dr. E. M. Christine Kris. She is the founder and director of M.I.N.D., the Multidisciplinary Institute for Neuropsychological Development, in Cambridge [Massachusetts]. She relates well to children, and she is a remarkable tester."

Vera went on to tell me that Dr. Kris had an even more unusual background than Vera had. Born in Austria, she attended private school in England prior to and during World War II. At the young age of 14, while still in high school, she was a linguist decoder for the British Intelligence and contributed to the breaking of the changing German codes. "I think," Vera concluded, "Dr. Kris can help Kelly and may be the one person who can solve the riddle of Brian."

I called Dr. Kris and learned from her that she was affiliated with Harvard and was a special education consultant to both public and private schools in New York and other New England states. Dr. Kris agreed to meet with us the very next week, and I set up an appointment for Kelly and another for Brian.

10

Kelly's Downhill Slide

"I go to school wearing a smile, but in my heart I'm dying."
—Kelly

In some families, brothers and sisters seem cut from the same cloth; in other families, like ours, each child seems unique, as though from a different family altogether. Kelly was always one of the most popular girls in her class, but she struggled academically. Whitney consistently got the highest or second-highest marks in her class, but she was far more reserved. Penny was a dreamer from the day she was born.

Kelly had been a beautiful, easy baby who did everything on schedule or ahead of schedule. She had walked before she was a year old and had then experimented with different walking styles: backward, sideways, and waddling like a duck. She had been outgoing, happy, and in perpetual motion. She had a wonderful memory for everything she saw, and she told you everything she saw and knew in great detail. She never just told you she had fun; she had to tell you everything she had done during the day.

By the time she entered nursery school, Kelly was self-confident and had lots of friends, although she rarely sat still and she did not enjoy doing puzzles, playing board games, or crayoning in coloring books. The only thing that seemed to be really difficult for her was understanding abstractions. If I asked Kelly, "What color is this?" she would answer, "What do you mean?" On the other hand, if I asked, "Is this red, blue, or green?" she could identify the color. Since she was only going into nursery school, this didn't seem too alarming.

The next year, as Kelly entered kindergarten, it didn't seem to matter that she was always bouncing around. It was true that I always had to keep an eye on her and she was always getting into difficult situations, some of which were positively dangerous, but she had an inquisitive mind and a talent for posing interesting questions and making connections rapidly. For instance, at the age of five, she had asked me, "When the baby [Penny] makes wee-wee in you, Mommy, where does it go?" At six, when she heard me say that a friend was pregnant, she commented, "More sex." I asked her, "What is sex?" "You know," she explained, "it's when a mommy and daddy make babies. You and daddy have done it four times and I was the first."

It was when Kelly was in first grade that I began to notice a change in her. She had neat penmanship, she did well in gym, art, and music, and she was popular, but she did not learn to read. Her spelling was atrocious, and her math skills were marginal. Early in the year, her teacher said, "Kelly can do the work if she just sits still and tries." Like most parents would, I told her to sit still and pay attention to the teacher. At the same time, however, memories of my own early problems with reading nudged their way into my mind. Although I did not recognize all the parallels between Kelly and myself, probably because I was so worried about Brian, I was troubled. I knew that once you have failed to learn one thing, you often fear other new learning situations and the more you fail, the more you feel different and inferior. I didn't want that to happen to Kelly, so I took her to be tested by Dr. Cole at Massachusetts General Hospital at the end of first grade.

Dr. Cole found that Kelly's auditory/visual memory was poor—she could not connect the few phonetic rules she knew to what was on the page. He suggested she work with the tutors at Ridge School during second grade. I talked to the school, and we arranged for tutoring sessions at school, which I tried to reinforce at home. The tutoring sessions at school helped but put Kelly in an awkward situation. She stayed in the classes that were most difficult for her and went for extra help during the classes she liked; consequently, she never felt that she was doing well. Second grade was not looking like a bright and shining year for Kelly, and the gloom deepened when I came to realize that she didn't understand basic math concepts.

Ridge School began teaching the multiplication tables in second grade. One Sunday afternoon, I asked to see her math homework. "I haven't done it because my answer book is at school," she said. By "answer book," she meant her math book, which had the multiplication tables printed in it. I immediately began to wonder how much she actually knew of multiplication. Her homework sheet contained problems like 35×5 equals __ and 65×10 equals __. Kelly, I discovered as soon as I sat down with her, had no idea what "something times something" even meant, let alone what the combination of numbers might equal. Without her book with the multiplication tables in it, of course, she couldn't come up with an answer.

I took her upstairs to her bedroom. On the floor, I made five stacks of books with five books in each stack. I said, "If we add together all the books in the five stacks, it is the same as multiplying 5×5."

Kelly didn't understand, wasn't interested, became angry as I said it again, and kicked the books all over the floor. For the next two hours, I tried to show her the connection between addition and multiplication, and she tried to leave the room. Each time I stopped her. Finally I said, "Neither of us is leaving until you understand the meaning of 5 × 5 and how much it equals." Kelly cried, threw things at me, dumped everything out of her dresser drawers, and finally climbed onto the windowsill and ran back and forth in front of the open window. The sill was like a balance beam, and there was a full-story drop to the tiled patio below. I didn't dare go near Kelly as she ran angrily along that narrow precipice. Finally, she grew tired and agreed to help me build stacks of books and count them.

That night as I lay in bed, I wondered if what I had put Kelly and myself through that afternoon had been worth it. Kelly now understood the difference between addition and multiplication, and she knew that 5 × 5 equals 25, but the afternoon had definitely put a strain on our relationship. What was it going to take for her to master the rest of the multiplication tables so that they would come to her as automatically as her own name? Her teachers certainly weren't getting through to her, and my explanations also didn't seem to bring immediate enlightenment. I knew she was intelligent. Everyone knew that. So, why was it so hard for her to understand reading and math? Kelly already hated her school tutoring sessions, so I hated to suggest tutoring in arithmetic.

We struggled on at home, improvising as we went. But the struggle at home and at school took its toll. She was learning to read, maybe not as well or as quickly as her classmates, but still she was reading. In the process, however, my beautiful Kelly, with her flowing light brown hair, hazel eyes, magnetic smile, and outgoing personality was losing confidence in herself.

By the middle of third grade, even with the progress she had made in reading and math, she was falling behind in school. Although she had many friends, she could not feel successful in the classroom, and without ever meaning to, Whitney was shaking Kelly's self-confidence still more. A year behind Kelly, Whitney soaked in great quantities of information and made it look easy. She was already an avid reader and devoured books several years more difficult than her grade level or Kelly's. Furthermore, she remembered all that she saw and heard.

Halfway through fourth grade, Kelly all but fell apart. Ridge School recommended that she see a psychiatrist at the Judge Baker Clinic. I took her to see a doctor there, who had her tested and asked to see her once a week. Kelly didn't like him, protested against going, and loathed the small room where she had to sit still and talk to him. "It's just like tutoring," she complained.

Although she hated it, the school felt it was the right thing for her, so I sent her once a week. By the time the end of the school year neared, she was utterly depressed, and it seemed to me the sessions only added to her misery. Throwing money at her problems didn't seem to be solving them.

It was at this time that I began to think that my daughter's difficulties might stem from some kind of perceptual impairment. The results of Dr. Scholl's neurological tests on Brian the previous fall, showing that he had some visual/motor/perceptual difficulty, had gotten me thinking about that a lot. Wasn't it possible that Kelly might have a type of perceptual impairment herself? Everyone had spent years telling her to pay attention, but perhaps no one had realized she *was* paying attention and trying to understand what others saw. Using this reasoning, it seemed clear to me that it was impossible for Kelly to achieve what was now demanded of her because she didn't have the concepts or skills she needed. And without those, I didn't see how anyone could build up her self-confidence.

When I called the psychiatrist and told him what I thought, he confessed that the psychological tester who had assessed Kelly at the very beginning had thought the same thing. I was stunned, and I reminded him furiously that I had asked for Kelly's test results months before. We had gone through months of therapy that totally ignored the problem. I finished our conversation by telling him that Kelly would not be continuing in therapy.

What Kelly really needed was help in understanding the process by which she learned. Once she understood that and her tutors understood it, too, nothing, I was sure, could stop her. At the moment, she was learning nothing at school, and she was so unhappy that she rarely invited children over.

In May 1968, one month before her tenth birthday, Kelly returned home from school in tears.

"Kelly what's wrong," I asked as I drew her into my arms.

"Oh, Mommy," she cried. "I go to school wearing a smile, but in my heart I'm dying."

I hugged her and tried to comfort her for several minutes. Then I asked, "Would you like to stop going to Ridge School and be tutored by a new tutor at home for the rest of the year? We can find a new school for you to go to next September."

"Do you mean I really don't have to go back to school this year?" she asked.

"That's right," I answered.

Kelly smiled and hugged me back. She looked happier than she had in months and kept saying, "Thank you, Mommy, thank you, thank you, thank you."

I notified Ridge and began the search for a new school. Luckily, I quickly found a retired tutor who was willing to work with Kelly at her home for the remainder of the school year. Each morning I dropped Kelly off at 9:30 and retrieved her at noon. After lunch she had an hour's homework, which had to pass my inspection before she could do anything else. Kelly was unpleasantly surprised to discover that my offer to take her out of school hadn't meant she could stop studying. She was upset at the nonstop tutoring. She missed her friends, also, and her years of frustration and defeat had badly damaged her self-image.

During the summer, Kelly went to overnight camp, and I arranged for her tutoring to continue while she was there. I instructed the tutor to conduct the lessons on beaches, during walks through the wooded areas, and in other outdoor settings. Beaches and dirt paths were wonderful chalkboards that did not smell of chalk and yet could be used to illustrate new problems. Long walks gave Kelly and her tutor a chance to discuss new material or make up cheers for spelling words.

In the fall, Kelly attended fifth grade in a Brookline public elementary school and was tutored at home in the afternoons by Vera Moretti. Kelly's class was using the identical books she had colored in and learned nothing from during the fourth grade at Ridge. Even that much familiarity with the books, however, put her on a more level footing with her new classmates.

Late that September, I took Kelly to see Dr. Kris a few days before Brian went for his testing. Dr. Kris found Kelly to be what we knew she was—very intelligent and hyperactive. She also had, Dr. Kris noted, a visual/perceptual problem. In some of the areas that were affected by this problem, Kelly had already taught herself how to compensate. When she had to copy a design, for example, she would use her hand to cover parts of the design. Then she would draw the part that was not blocked, move her hand and draw another part, until the design was completed.

Well, I thought, we are beginning to uncover the problems, and she is coping with them. Perhaps the tutoring will allow her to catch up, especially now that we have a better handle on the problems. It took time to fill in the gaps, and there were very difficult periods, but I was right. Once Kelly was started on the right track, nothing could stop her.

11

Games Give Brian Space and Time

"Where is Wednesday, inside or out?"

—Brian

For many years, Brian didn't progress greatly unless he and I progressed together. Before he could gain a new skill, I had to figure out all the little steps involved in the skill and then feed this information into him in meager spoonfuls. Such spoonfuls of learning applied to all our at-home tutoring sessions. When I first undertook teaching Brian in a concerted manner, I told him we were going to play a game. The early games were very simple. To teach the concepts of "less" and "more," for example, I used two small boxes, three large paper plates, and several toy cars. I couldn't just put some cars on a plate, and a few less on another, and say "This is more and this is less." It didn't mean anything to Brian. He had to be able to touch less or more, and he had to start with one idea, "less," and then build up to the other idea, "more."

I had Brian spread the plates out in a straight line in front of us. I pointed to the middle plate and had him place one car on it. Then I pointed to the plate on his right and asked him to place the rest of the cars on that plate. I explained that the empty plate didn't have any cars on it, so it had less cars than each of the other plates. Then I asked Brian which plates had more cars than the empty plate. Then I asked him to look at the two plates with cars and tell me which plate had more than the other plate. Each time Brian responded correctly to a problem, he'd put a pretzel in his box, which was labeled "Brian." If he gave an incorrect response, I placed a pretzel in my box, labeled "Mom."

As the nights went on, I changed the number of cars on the plates, added plates, had Brian order the plates, and introduced more complex concepts. Sometimes we made garages out of the plates and played the same games placing the cars in the garages rather than on the plates. Because of his very short attention span, he needed constant variety, but the variety still had to be broken into steps. At the end of each session, we counted our pretzels to see who had the most. Brian always won.

These games, however, were about the only games Brian could win or even play. Games with his sisters usually ended in bursts of rage on his part or tears on their part. As Kelly struggled with fourth grade, I watched Brian try to join in when Whitney and her friends played Candy Land and Chutes and Ladders. I marveled at his persistent demands to play as he refused to play by the rules and inevitably quit in frustration before the game was over. When they let him try, he insisted upon going first, even if there were rules for determining who should be first. He moved his marker without spinning the spinner or drawing a card. When it was someone else's turn, he said they took "too long." When it was his turn, he sometimes moved his opponent's marker or forgot which direction his marker should move. Sometimes he counted the space on which his marker rested as space one. Given the chaos that resulted every time he tried to play, I couldn't imagine why he wanted to, but he did, and

I worried that he would give up if he couldn't succeed eventually.

As I tried to teach him how to play these games, I began to understand why they always resulted in rages. Brian didn't understand the basic concepts these games required, such as left and right, sequence, progression, "turn" (including who goes first), and "winning." Indeed, Brian seemed to be unaware of his own body's relation to anything else. Was that one reason he ran through the dining room knocking over the chairs, so he could know where he was in relation to them? Probably because of my own poor sense of direction, I thought about Brian's perception of where he was in space. I knew that when I didn't know where I was, I found it impossible to know how to get to a particular place from there. How could Brian move a marker in a logical progression if he didn't know where he was in relation to his marker? How could he play the game if he didn't know where his marker had to move to get to "home"? Location and sequence seemed to be the key words. Every night I laid out Brian's clothes for him—underpants, undershirt, shirt, and pants. Every night I told him to start *here*—with his underpants— and work his way down the row in the morning when he got dressed. If I didn't, he was just as likely to start with his shirt and end up with his underpants over his pants.

I wasn't sure where my mental monologue was getting me, so I turned my thoughts back to Kelly as a preschooler. I remembered that she either couldn't or didn't want to play Candy Land and Chutes and Ladders, but she did occasionally play Hi-Ho! Cherry-O, although she didn't seem to enjoy it. For weeks I thought about those games. What were the differences in concepts and skills required to play Hi-Ho! Cherry-O, Candy Land, and Chutes and Ladders? It turned out that Hi-Ho! Cherry-O required only two steps by its players. The players flicked the spinner and then matched the number on the spinner to the number of cherries they could take off the tree. In Candy Land and Chutes and Ladders, however, players could move forward or backward on the board, and at the same time they could sit anywhere around the board (requiring additional understanding of where your body is in space). Spinners were used to get a number, but then players used that number to count spaces on the board. Hi-Ho! Cherry-O was a one-to-one matching game; in the other games there was no one-to-one match, and a player moved forward or backward in no obvious sequence.

Over the years, I've discovered my brain frequently continues to deal with a problem while I'm asleep at night. Often when I had gone through several days in which Brian and I seemed to be at a standstill, I would awake during the night with a solution to the problem. I continued to mull over the game problem. Finally, one night I awoke around 2:00 A.M. with an idea for a new game. I knew the rules, and I knew how the playing surface and playing pieces should look. I even knew that I would use special starting pieces that would locate Brian in space. In this game, Brian would sit in a specific place with his track on the board directly in front of him. The spaces on his track would be positioned in single file outward from where he was sitting. I would sit next to him in front of my own track, and we would fill in each space on our own track as we moved toward our goals—no blank spaces, no possibility of becoming confused about the direction to go in. The winner would get a pretzel, so "win" meant getting a pretzel.

I quietly got out of bed, threw on a pair of jeans and a sweat shirt, collected some cardboard, and went to the family room. By 5:30 that morning, when Brian awoke, I'd finished making the starting pieces, the playing board, and the cards. I grabbed twenty cars, a card holder, and a trophy from our large toy closet, and a box of straight pretzels from the kitchen. These were the playing pieces for the game. Then, I took the game into Brian's room to try it out. He was anxious to play. The first time we played, I won and immediately took the pretzel from the trophy on the playing board and ate it.

Brian, of course, wanted a pretzel, too, but I told him he would have to win the game to get one. He was furious but finally agreed to play again. I put another pretzel in the trophy. This time he won and immediately snatched the pretzel and ate it. By the end of the day, he had learned what it meant to "win" and to "lose." He had also learned to change his reaction of anger at losing to "Let's play again."

After Brian and I had played this game for several days and he had become very proficient at it, he played it with his sisters. Both his performance and behavior were the standard five- to six-year-old ones, and I glowed inside.

My sense of ecstacy was short lived, however. A few days later, Whitney came running down the hall in tears, and I could hear Brian in a rage in the family room. She blurted out, "I let him play Chutes and Ladders with Ellie and me, and he kept moving his marker to the wrong space, so we finally told him he couldn't play. Now he's torn up the playing board and spinner and is throwing the pieces all over the room."

I removed Brian to his bedroom, where he continued to wail for another hour, and distracted the girls with a finger-painting kit. By dinner time, after I had picked up Kelly from her dance lesson and bathed Penny, life was semi-normal again, but my glow over Brian's behavior a few days earlier had faded. I wondered if my efforts to teach him board games were misdirected.

Somehow I found the courage to follow my initial gut instincts and purchase two new Chutes and Ladders games, one for Whitney and her friends and the other for Brian and me. That night, during quiet time with Brian in his bedroom, I tried to play Chutes and Ladders with him again. This time I really studied his behavior. By his third turn, I had discovered that he didn't understand abstract sequencing—moving one piece from space to space rather than filling in spaces with pieces as he did in my game. I knew then that I needed to elaborate upon the game I had developed. I told Brian that it was getting late and that I didn't have time to finish the game but I had a surprise for him. I gave him a new little toy car, tucked him in bed, and rubbed his back, and we escaped without the usual tears.

Over the next six months, I developed new games, each based on the initial game and each making location, progression, and sequence more abstract. I soon learned that when I developed a game that Brian didn't understand, he'd say, "I don't like this game" or "I don't want to play this game, it's not fun." These comments told me that I hadn't fed in the correct next step, so I would go back to the last game he had liked and try a different variation. As we sat on the floor next to each other playing the games, Brian's comments would help me discover the correct next step. Eventually, Brian could sit anywhere around one board with other players and other markers, flick a spinner, and move his marker either forward or backward while always trying to reach the winner's spot.

The games improved Brian's spatial orientation, helped his matching and basic arithmetic skills, developed his ability to sequence, and gave him a relatively quiet activity to enjoy with others. As a result, he matured intellectually and socially. Even when he could play Candy Land, Chutes and Ladders, and other commercially available games with his sisters and friends, he continued to play the games I had developed for several years, and within two years of our first game, he was able to play chess and other adult games.

Developing and playing the games with Brian had been challenging and fun for both of us, but I soon discovered Penny also liked them. Penny was in a nursery school for four-year-olds during my game-making days, so she joined in when Brian and I played. One day I received a call from a neighbor asking me where she could buy the games with the pretzels that her four-year-old daughter played at our house. Unbeknownst to me, Penny had taught her friends to play these games. My neighbor's call made me realize that the board games were appropriate for all preschoolers, not just children with problems.

Several years later, I wrote a rule book embracing nine games and a separate instructor's guide to accompany them. For a brief period after obtaining three patents on them, I hoped to market the games, but I couldn't convince toy companies and publishers to manufacture and distribute them. Finally, I produced 100 copies, which were called "The 1, 2, 3 Instructional Program." (My children and their friends still call them "The Pretzel Games," their original title.) Some 80 of these were sold by a large hospital supplier trying to break into the special education market. I lost money and the company made $25 on each set of games it sold. When the company ran out of games but declined to help finance additional copies, I took the 1, 2, 3 Instructional Program off the market. I donated some of the remaining sets to special education facilities and stored a few for prospective grandchildren. (If any reader is interested in the games, I'd be delighted to let him or her run with the ball. I know they are worthwhile and still think with proper marketing they can be financially successful.)

As Brian's game playing ability improved, I began to think about his inability to understand time. When he was nearly six years old, he still seemed unable to grasp when a future event would occur. One morning he asked me ten times in twenty minutes when he was going to a birthday party. The first nine times I answered with the best description I could give, but the tenth time, I said, "Brian, the party is tomorrow, which is Wednesday. Now, you will have to believe me and don't ask me that again."

Brian looked at me and asked, "Where is Wednesday, inside or out? I'll believe you when you show it to me."

His question made me realize that my explanations had meant nothing to him. He had no understanding of where he was in time, just as earlier he had not known where he was in space.

That night, as it turned out, was the night I left on a trip that was to start with a visit with Cristina in Spain. During dinner on the long flight, I wondered how I was going to show Brian Wednesday. After the flight attendant cleared away my dinner tray, I fell asleep. An hour later I awoke with the answer to "Where is Wednesday?"

Brian, I knew, understood "now": I want the brownie NOW. I want to go out and play NOW. I don't want to go to bed NOW. For him there seemed to be no past or future—only the immediate present. Because he understood "now" and learned things more easily when he could physically touch them, I would devise a calendar to help him record his "nows" so that he could view them in their sequence within the structure of a day.

For Brian, as for most children, I thought, a day consisted of five fixed activities—getting up in the morning, eating three meals, and going to bed at night. Therefore, these activities along with the name of each day of the week would be permanent features on his calendar. At the top of each day on the calendar, there would be an empty space into which Brian would place a picture of himself with the word "TODAY" on it. Under that space would be the name of a day. Under Sunday (or whichever day of the week it was) would be the permanent picture of a boy getting out of bed. Beneath the picture of the boy getting out of bed there would be an empty space to record the weather, then a picture of breakfast and three empty spaces to record morning activities. The picture of lunch would be followed by three more empty spaces to record afternoon activities. A space between dinner and going to bed would let him insert his evening activity. Each day I'd have Brian place pictures of his "nows" between the permanent features in eight empty spaces.

I spent several hours drawing the calendar, which Cristina suggested I have built in Spain. I explained to the carpenter we found that I needed a large wooden frame attached to a sheet of steel. Vertically the frame was to be divided into seven columns, one for each day of the week. There would be fourteen horizontal rows, five of which would ultimately contain the permanent pictures and nine of which would be empty to allow pictures in small magnetic frames to be inserted and removed.

A month later the calendar was flown to New York by a pilot whose children attended Cristina's school. A friend of mine retrieved the calendar at Kennedy and brought it to Boston in her van. It took another two months to make the small magnetic picture frames, to complete the artwork, and to paint the calendar. Now all was ready.

I waited for a Sunday morning to give Brian his new calendar. It was quiet in our house except for the noises Brian was making as he imitated the sounds of cars and planes while he played. I lugged the heavy calendar into his room and announced I'd made a new game, called "Brian's Calendar."

I handed him a picture of himself labeled TODAY, which I'd already put in a magnetic frame, and instructed him to place it in the top left empty space on the calendar. Beneath the space in which he placed his picture the word "SUNDAY" was written. I pointed to the picture below the word "SUNDAY," which showed a boy getting out of bed, and I asked, "What is the first thing you do each day?" He looked at me and at the calendar and said, "I get out of bed."

"That's right," I said, "just like the boy on your calendar. This marks the beginning of day." Then I told Brian to look out the window and identify, just as he did in Rosalie's class, whether he saw sun, clouds, rain, or snow in the sky. He saw the sun, so I showed him the storage space that housed many pictures, including seven suns, seven rains, seven clouds, and seven snow scenes. I told Brian to take one of the suns and place it in the space under the boy getting out of bed. As Brian got dressed, we talked about how people frequently wear different clothes when they go outside, depending on what they see in the sky.

The picture below the sun showed a boy eating breakfast, so we ate breakfast. Afterward we returned to Brian's room and talked about what he would do next. He wanted to go out and ride his bike, so I asked him to find a picture of a boy riding a bike in the calendar's storage cabinet and to place it in the empty spot under the picture of a boy eating breakfast. Later that morning, when Brian played with blocks, he put a picture of a boy playing with blocks under the picture of the boy riding a bike.

When John Green, Brian's friend, came over, I took a Polaroid picture of John, cut it to the size of the magnetic frame, and Brian placed John's picture on his calendar as the final event of the morning. Below John's picture was the picture of a boy eating lunch, which we did. During the afternoon, the boys put pictures of their afternoon activities on the calendar as they did them.

Finally we reached the picture of a boy eating dinner with an empty space below it and then the picture of a boy going to bed. Brian ate dinner, placed a picture of a TV in his evening space, and then climbed into bed. As we talked before I turned out the light, I explained that this first column was Brian's day, which was also called Sunday and today.

The next morning I had Brian move his picture to the closest empty space to the right of Sunday. Below TODAY was now written MONDAY, which I pointed out and explained. We followed the same procedure each day throughout the week. Saturday night, just before Brian was about to climb into bed, I explained that the week was over, and we placed all the removable pictures back in storage except for Brian's picture, which we left at the top of Saturday. The following morning Brian placed his picture above Sunday, and we began another week.

Slowly but surely, Brian came to understand the concepts and sequence of "morning," "afternoon," "evening," "today," "day," "night," and that "today" and "day" can also have names like Sunday, Monday, Tuesday, Wednesday, Thursday, Friday, and Saturday. Later, using the calendar, Brian learned the meaning of "yesterday" and "tomorrow" and what a week consists of. When he understood these, I introduced Brian to the concept of a month—a series of days in a series of weeks. Ultimately, Brian mastered the abstract identifying features of a given day—Sunday, June 26, 1968, for example.

It has now been over twenty-five years since I invented the games and calendar that solved riddles for Brian about space, time, and sequencing—prerequisites for much other learning. Yet, today, all these years later, even though the educational and scientific communities understand these processes, the appropriate remediation is often not used.

An interviewer once reported that Einstein, when asked how he had come up with the theory of relativity, had replied, "I sometimes ask myself, how did it come that I was the one to develop the theory of relativity? The reason, I think, is that a normal adult never stops to think about problems of space and time. These are things which he has thought of as a child. But my intellectual development was retarded, as a result of which I began to wonder about space and time only when I had already grown up. Naturally, I could go deeper into the problem than a child with normal ability."

It is curious that Brian and I had to learn about space, time, and sequencing at a later age than usual, but we did. And it became clear to me as Brian mastered these concepts that he needed them before many other kinds of learning could take place. In fact, what I've come to realize is that all children need these concepts and skills as the building blocks for more advanced learning.

12

Struggling within the System

"If you love me, please come and get me out of here."

—Brian

There are hidden costs to being the mother of a learning-disabled child, especially when the child is hyperactive. These costs are multiplied when you have more than one child with learning disabilities. In some ways, the worry never ends. Of course, you always worry about your children, whether or not there are learning problems, but there are times when you get a break in your worry: you go off and play tennis because your children are at school and they'll be fine there. You don't spend your days planning how to teach reading or math or even wondering if your child will ever read. You don't spend your evenings wondering where your child will go to school next and if anyone will break through what appears to be an insurmountable barrier.

During the summer of 1968, before Kelly's and Brian's first visits with Dr. Kris, I had seen signs that Brian, with the help of Ritalin, was learning to control bursts of rage when things didn't go right. Cars had always fascinated him, and he knew the makes and models of most cars on the road and had begun to extend his interest to airplanes. Although he still couldn't write his name, he loved building model planes from kits. He couldn't read the directions, but he intuitively fit the many pieces together and studied the drawings when he couldn't guess where a piece was to go.

One day, as I passed the playroom where he was building a model plane, I heard him exclaim, "S—t!" I marched into the room saying, "Brian!" He responded with an angry, "Sorry." "What's the matter?" I asked. "I glued the wrong two parts together," he explained, "and now I can't get them apart."

To myself I thought, No two ways about it, swearing is a big improvement on raging rampages around the house. Combining this with Brian's increasing understanding of space and time, I found myself thinking first grade might go better than I had expected.

A few days before the fall term began at Heath School, I learned that the first grade teacher I had chosen had become pregnant and would not be returning. Because I didn't know Terry Cerra, the new teacher, I called Rosalie Richardson, who agreed to have Brian return to her class for the first few weeks of school. During this time I wanted to observe Terry, who, I felt, needed a chance to settle in with her new group before taking on Brian.

Terry, I soon discovered, was a "born" teacher. She was young and caring, and I immediately liked her and knew she would be good with Brian. At our conference, she suggested that she observe Brian in Rosalie's special education class and get pointers for teaching him from Rosalie. Shortly thereafter she visited Rosalie's class and met Brian. They also liked each other immediately, and so in mid-October Brian transferred from Rosalie's special education class to Terry's first grade.

Before Brian transferred to Terry's class, we met with Dr. Kris. Kelly's appointment had been a few days earlier; at ten years old, she had been an interested and willing participant. When I arrived with Brian, he was six and a half years old and not easy to test. He had been tested so much that sometimes he would tell a doctor what card he would see next in the test. This seemed to pose no problem to Dr. Kris, who had a wonderful way of gaining his confidence and keeping him happy but under control. At the end of the testing, Dr. Kris went over the results with me. I cried as she told me Brian had a receptive IQ of 130 and that, with proper help, Brian's future was promising. How long had I waited and hoped for those words!

Once I regained my composure, Dr. Kris explained to me that Brian had severe eye-hand, eye-foot coordination problems; visual/perceptual problems, meaning, to put it simplistically, he didn't see objects, including letters, as most people did, nor did his mind always translate what he saw as most people's minds did; and a "language unscrambling" problem. She also noted that he had sequencing and organizational problems. She gave me so much information that I could hardly take all of it in. She then suggested concepts and skills I should teach Brian at specific stages of his development.

We began with gymnastic mats and balance beams so he could work on his coordination, then we moved on to all sorts of manipulative objects, so he could improve his fine motor coordination. When Dr. Kris later suggested that Brian should learn how to skip, I figured out the steps involved in skipping. I was used to thinking this way, having developed the games and the calendar for Brian. To skip, you take a step, hop on one foot, take a step, and hop on the other foot. First Brian had to be able to hop on one foot, which meant being able to balance on one foot. Once he achieved that, then he had to be able to hop on the other foot and put the sequence together—step, hop, step, hop. This was the process by which he finally learned to skip, at age seven.

After our first appointment with Dr. Kris, I wrote lesson plans every day for Brian to take in to Terry in the morning because he lacked the basic skills to cope with much of the first-grade curriculum. I also sent along the specially lined paper from Cove School as Brian needed the color-cued lines to know where to write his letters.

One day when I arrived before the end of the school day, I observed Brian's class from a window. There was Brian, frequently interrupting, demanding special help, often unable to follow directions, and frequently not getting the point, partly because he couldn't wait long enough to hear all the directions and partly because he thought so concretely. I marveled at Terry's patience and talent for keeping him constructively busy while coping with twenty-four other youngsters. I knew only too well how difficult it was to teach Brian when he was alone, not to mention when others were around. His concrete thinking and language unscrambling problems in themselves made it a challenge.

As an example, one night, as I worked to improve Brian's grasp of number concepts, I had handed him two sheets of colored paper. Beforehand, I had divided each colored sheet into four equal rectangles. In the top left rectangle of each page, I had pasted pictures of five little boats. Six small trucks were in each of the top right squares, seven planes in each of the bottom left squares, and eight go-carts in each of the bottom right squares. On one sheet, I had drawn a line under the six small trucks and then folded that paper in half vertically and horizontally. I now handed Brian the folded and unfolded sheets.

"Brian," I said, "one rectangle has six objects in it. Draw a line under those six objects. When you have finished, open up the other page and see if you have drawn the line in the same place where I drew mine."

Brian sat staring at the opened page and doing nothing. Finally he picked up the folded page and turned it over and over in his hands.

I was becoming frustrated. "Brian, do you know how many six is?"

"Yes," he said. He continued turning the folded page in his hands.

I was about to take it away from him when he said, "I don't know how you got your line under the six small trucks without tearing the paper."

By "under" Brian had understood me to say between the stickers of the six trucks and the sheet of paper to which they were affixed. He knew the math but didn't understand that "under" could also mean "below."

Another time I had taken him with me when I went to the Ridge School library to pick up assignments and books for Whitney, who was home with the flu. I needed something for Brian to do while I got the books from the stacks. On a table in the center of the library I noticed a record player with a head set. I sat Brian down at the table, put on a record about the life of Leonardo da Vinci, and put the earphones on Brian. As I searched for Whitney's books, returning every few minutes to check on Brian, bells rang, kids rushed back and forth, and Brian sat glued to the earphones. It had taken me half an hour to collect all the books, and during that time Brian had sat quietly listening to the record over and over. It was the longest I had ever seen him sit still.

In the car coming home, as he recited features of Leonardo's life to me in great detail, I had suddenly realized how much more he could learn when he didn't have to contend with any background noise or stimulation. But that wasn't possible, and Brian would have to learn how to cope.

Many weeknights Terry and I spoke by phone. This allowed both of us to have a picture of Brian's learning and behavior at home and at school. It also kept me abreast of what the class was doing. In that way, I could keep Brian's assignments on the level at which he could succeed and, whenever possible, tie them into what his peers were doing. I knew it frustrated him that he was the only student in his class who couldn't read. On the other hand, being in a normal classroom allowed him to develop friendships with several classmates, improve his athletic skills and receive peer recognition for them, and achieve some academic progress.

Even with this progress, however, Brian continued exhibiting bizarre behavior in certain situations. In first grade, he was still terrified of having his hair cut. Since I couldn't hold his head still and cut his hair at the same time, we went to a barber. We would arrive at the little salon and be warmly welcomed by gray-haired, good-natured Emilio, who would always greet us with, "Well, what's it going to be today, Brian?"

If I wasn't holding onto his hand tightly, Brian would try to hide behind the coats hanging on the coat rack in the corner. The only way he would get into the chair was if I sat there first. Emilio would put a cover on me, then cover Brian as he sat on my lap. Although Brian would squirm, he would allow Emilio to cut his hair with a scissors. Electrical clippers were impossible as he would scream and shake his head furiously. Brian could never explain why he was so fearful of the clippers, but I had the feeling he was oversensitive to the noise rather than afraid he would get cut. I demonstrated the use of the clippers on the palm of my hand the first few times we went, but it didn't change Brian's behavior. By the end of the session, hair was everywhere, even in my shoes.

❖ ❖ ❖

Brian moved on to second grade still behind his peers. The second grade consisted of thirty-five youngsters divided into two groups, one of twenty-five and one of ten. Brian was one of the ten children crammed into an unusually tiny classroom. His teacher had read all the books, but she knew nothing about children nor how they learn. I found she would not listen to me, which was frustrating, but worse, she would not even listen to the recommendations of our pediatrician, Dr. Berenberg.

As the year progressed, Brian displayed his frustration with school in outbursts of anger. He made little academic progress that year, despite my daily teaching sessions and despite the efforts of Susan Volpe, his capable private tutor at home who had replaced Vera Moretti. (Vera had finally had to admit she couldn't handle both her work at Fernald and tutoring Kelly and Brian).

The one saving grace of that year was Brian's new friendship with David Silver. On the surface, these two youngsters were very different: David was small; Brian was big. David had a large vocabulary and expressed himself well; Brian mispronounced words ("hopsical" for *hospital*, "aks" for *ask*, "sues" for *shoes*, "sua" for *sure*) and had poor syntax. David was predictable and reliable; no one ever knew what Brian was going to do next. Both boys were bright, yet each excelled in the area in which the other, at that time, was least competent. Brian's successes were in athletics; David would later become a champion ice skater, but at seven, he was too small to be competitive with his larger classmates. Brian was at the bottom of his class academically; David was at the top. Even so, an understanding and respect for one another developed and grew. Today, they are still close friends. David, now a doctor, is married to a young woman who was introduced to him by Brian.

Still, the year's saving grace of his friendship with David did not help Brian academically. I finally decided, with great misgivings, to send Brian to boarding school for third grade. I visited several and with fingers crossed, I chose a school I will call Hampton. It was a boarding school for learning-disabled boys, and the director was well thought of in educational circles. Unfortunately, he left at the same time Brian arrived, and the remaining administrators disagreed about educational policy and the direction of the school.

Brian and I were stoic when we parted at the start of the school year, but once I was in the car the tears flowed, and at night when passing his empty, neatly made bed, the tears would again run down my cheeks. Weekend visits left me uneasy about the school. I found myself explaining teaching techniques I had seen at Cove School or Crotched Mountain School. Shortly before Thanksgiving, Brian called home and summed up the situation: "This place looks like a camp because it has a gym and lots of playing fields, but it's not fun, so it's not a camp. It feels like a school because it has class-rooms, teachers, and books, but I'm not learning anything, so it's not a school. If you love me, please come and get me out of here."

I arrived at the school in less than two hours and found Brian and another youngster sitting in the rain on the curb at the school's entrance. They were both drenched, and Brian was covered from head to toe with a rash. I was horrified to discover that no one was aware the boys had missed their last two activities and had been sitting in the rain for over an hour, or that Brian had had a rash for several days. Arriving unex-pectedly gave me the chance to see that the sanitary condi-tions were despicable, the classrooms and dorms were in disorder, and supervision, at best, was loose. Angry with myself for having sent him there, I promptly withdrew him from the school, brought him home, started tutoring him again, and undertook the search for another school.

We again visited several. The most impressive was Linden Hill in Northfield, Massachusetts, but I was afraid to send Brian off again immediately. I finally chose Krebs School in nearby Lexington. It was a small special educational day school that looked more like a home. It was run by Ida Krebs, a warm, motherly woman, who took youngsters with a vari-ety of problems. The school's only drawback, to my mind, was its lack of athletic teams or gym classes. To fill this gap, I sent Brian to a sports program at The Academy in Newton Center a few afternoons each week. Brian needed plenty of exercise, physical as well as mental, and I knew that it was his athletic ability that would gain him peer recognition when he returned to a regular classroom.

Brian's teacher eased his transition into Krebs School nice-ly and provided work that stimulated him but was within his reach. The year, which had looked very bleak, became a happy, productive one, and Brian made several new friends.

His best friend at the school was a girl named Jody. They were the same age, and both were hyperactive, bright, had learning disabilities, and took Ritalin.

One Saturday, the two were playing at our house and being particularly wild—running, falling, and smashing into everything. At lunch Brian said to me, "Please give Jody one of my pills. Her mother forgot to give her Ritalin this morning, and I can't stand her!" I promptly called Jody's mother, who said yes, she had forgotten, and asked me to give Jody one of Brian's 5 mg Ritalin tablets.

Later that afternoon, I heard Jody screaming at Brian, "I hate you! I want to go home and I'm never going to play with you again!" I ran to the playroom, fully expecting disaster. I found Jody in one piece but crying her heart out. They had been wrestling on the gymnastic mats, and Brian had taken the opportunity to kiss her. "I'm really sorry. I promise never to kiss you again," Brian pleaded with tears beginning to well up in his eyes. It seemed like a good time for a break. They ate snacks and then played happily for the rest of the afternoon.

Unfortunately, Brian's fourth-grade teacher was not as good as his third-grade teacher had been. By spring term, Brian was saying that he wasn't learning anything at school and that I had better start tutoring him again, which I did, and began the search for still another school.

13

The Right School Makes the Difference

The letter a says (ă) as in apple, (ā) as in baby, and (â) as in all.

—Gillingham / Stillman

Brian was listening when Mr. Hayes, the headmaster of Linden Hill School, said, "If you come to Linden Hill, you will not go home until your work is completed to my satisfaction. You have a problem that I can show you how to solve."

We had gone to visit the school again after Brian finished fourth grade. Mr. Hayes went on to tell Brian that only those boys who were ready to work on solving their problems were admitted to Linden Hill. No boy was accepted just because his parents wanted him out of the house. Thus, only with Mr. Hayes's okay would Brian be allowed to return home anytime, including Christmas, spring vacation, and summer vacation. Mr. Hayes warned Brian that he would have to work harder than he had ever worked before, but through this work, he would learn to read and do the things he wanted to do. Finally, he had said to Brian, "Go home and think about what you want to do. If you decide to come to Linden Hill, you, not your parents, must call me."

During our drive home, Brian had confided, "I know I should go to Linden Hill, but I'm afraid I will stay there for the rest of my life." I assured him that if he did what he was told to do, he would always be allowed to return home during vacations.

Immediately after we arrived home, Brian had asked me to write down Mr. Hayes's number. After I had done this, he went to the phone and dialed the number. His call was brief. "Mr. Hayes, I'm coming to your school."

Mr. Hayes must have responded that he looked forward to having him because two minutes later Brian was dialing his friend, David Silver. Brian asked me if David could come over and if I would pick him up now. The boys sat talking in the back seat of the car as we drove home.

I couldn't help but overhear their conversation. "You know I look normal but act retarded when I try to do the work in school," Brian said. "I've decided to go to a boarding school so I can learn like you do, but I'm worried about our never being together. If I don't do my work the way they want me to, I'm not allowed to come home for vacations."

"We'll always be friends, Brian," David answered. "The most important thing is that you go to a school where you can learn, and if they don't let you out I'll just come visit you there."

I had been thankful I was alone in the front seat so they couldn't see my tears. Now he was packing his suitcase and we were arguing over his baby pillow.

"You can't take that," I said as he tucked it next to his clothes. "You're ten years old. The other boys will tease you."

Brian simply pointed out that his baby pillow had a special smell and that he couldn't sleep without it. It was hard to argue with that statement. From the time he was two until he was about eleven, he had an extraordinary sense of smell. On more than one occasion, he had shown me his fire engine minutes before I heard an engine responding to a fire. After he had begun talking intelligibly, he would tell me he smelled smoke before we even heard the engines on the street below our house. I never smelled the smoke.

We compromised, and he took the case for his baby pillow, which he claimed had the desired smell. He kept it under his standard size pillow, and at night when it was dark and no one could see, he would put it under his head on top of the larger pillow.

After his first boarding school fiasco, I had serious reservations about sending him away to school, but Linden Hill was run as a family. The school had twenty boys, mostly ten- to twelve-year-olds, and it kept the number as close to twenty as possible in order to carry out the family strategy. The boys shared the responsibility of cleaning their own rooms and the school bus, collecting eggs from the chickens, cutting the grass on the soccer field, and waiting on tables.

Knowing Brian was going to be in a family environment that was structured reassured me somewhat. Children need warmth and structure to feel loved, and at Linden Hill, a boy always knew where he stood. I liked that. If Brian wasn't going to be with me, it was important that his environment be one that I felt comfortable with.

All the boys at the school were required to attend meals, wear coats and ties, and eat everything on their plate. They took turns serving the family-style meals. Fresh flowers decorated the dining room tables during the day, and there were candles on the tables at night. During the winter months, a large fire in the dining room fireplace warmed the boys as they ate. On our visit there, the fire had reminded me of the dinners my parents and I shared on cold, stormy, winter nights when I was young. My mother would put up a card table in the den, my father would make a large fire, and I would feel secure eating with them in front of the crackling fire as snow fell outside.

On Sundays and holidays, the cook at Linden Hill always prepared a turkey dinner with all the trimmings and equal to the finest Thanksgiving dinner served anywhere. Even at lunch the day of Brian's interview, the smell and taste of the roast chicken, served with peas, rice, and gravy, had left a succulent and favorable impression.

There were many rules, all of which were strictly enforced, but there were also incentives to encourage the boys. Rewards were given for outstanding achievement and for extra effort. The boys at Linden Hill were exposed to a way of life stressing specific values, a superb academic base, and excellent athletic (soccer and judo) instruction. The boys would read and understand *The Iliad* and other classics. Their readings were then supplemented by Mr. Hayes's lectures. He captivated the boys; they would listen spellbound as he related the Greek myths. Because the boys were all poor readers, they also saw films of many classics, such as *A Tale of Two Cities*, to help them broaden their literary base.

It didn't take long for a new boy to learn that there was no beating the system at Linden Hill. All the boys knew the consequences for each broken rule, and the boy who broke a rule was always the loser. Prior to Linden Hill, the boys were used to getting attention and their own way through disruptive or antisocial behavior. They were good at avoiding rather than learning what was required. Linden Hill provided an environment in which each boy knew what was expected of him and came to know that he could not avoid doing what was expected.

One boy who had disrupted his class with spitballs learned that the hard way. One Saturday night, when the youngster was set to leave the school bus to go to the movies with his classmates, Mr. Hayes told him he was going to spend his movie time on the bus practicing his favorite activity. Placing a pile of newspapers on a seat in the middle of the bus and a bucket in the aisle in the front of the bus, Mr. Hayes told the youngster to start making spitballs and spit them into the bucket. To make sure the boy did as he was told, Mr. Hayes stayed on the bus and read. After this, there were no more spitballs or conversation about them by the boy or his friends.

Once a boy actually realized that he could learn, the battle was half won. Mr. Hayes then pushed each boy to help him advance as quickly as possible, but he was never unreasonable in his demands. He knew what each boy could do and made sure they did it. I liked Mr. Hayes and felt that Brian would come to respect him. In fact, Mr. Hayes was the strong male role model I had wanted to find for Brian, who was growing up in a family primarily made up of women—three sisters, mostly female help, and a strong mother.

The first time I visited Brian after he started school at Linden Hill, he took me to the soccer field behind his single-story dorm and proudly demonstrated his newly acquired ball-handling skills. Then, still kicking the ball, he ran from the playing field, past the main house to the front lawn as I followed along at his side. When we arrived at the school's pond, Brian stopped to see if any ducks were swimming in it. His foot resting on the soccer ball, he looked up at me, smiled, and said, "Mr. Hayes has rules you haven't even thought of!"

"Like what?" I inquired.

"At night we are given a ten-minute warning before we have to be in bed with our light out. At the end of the ten minutes, there is a countdown, and anyone who still has his light on loses his light bulb."

I smiled and asked, "What other rules do you have here?"

"If a boy wets his bed, his sheets and mattress are thrown out the window. When they are dry, he has to get them back in his room and make his bed to pass inspection."

"Do you think that's fair?" I asked, curious to know his answer.

"You bet," Brian said. "Why should the rest of us have to put up with the smell of urine?"

"What do you do on weekends?" I inquired.

"Saturdays, we have soccer games. In the winter, we will go skiing. Saturday nights, we shower and go on the school bus, along with Mr. and Mrs. Hayes and our teachers, to a restaurant and then to a movie. What we get to eat depends on how we did in school during the week."

"What do you mean?" I asked.

"Boys who have worked hard all week and finished their assignments on time get enough money to buy a hamburger with french fries and cole slaw, a glass of milk, and a large hot fudge sundae. That's what I eat every Saturday night," he said with a smile.

"What happens to the boys who haven't completed their work properly?" I asked.

"If someone does an okay job during the week but less than what he can do, he gets enough money to have the same meal but with an ice cream cone instead of the hot fudge sundae. If a boy doesn't do his work (which almost never happens), he only gets enough for a glass of milk, a large bowl of soup, and some crackers."

During one of my visits to the school, I found no toilet paper in any of the bathrooms. When Brian got out of class, I asked him about it. He said, "Go ask Mr. Hayes for your ration."

"What are you talking about?" I asked.

"One of the boys is stuffing lots of toilet paper in the toilets so they overflow. Until Mr. Hayes learns who is doing it, there will be no toilet paper in the bathrooms. Each morning we line up and are given toilet paper that measures the same length as we are tall. If we need more paper, we have to go to Mr. Hayes and ask for it."

I found Mr. Hayes and said I'd like my ration. He smiled and handed me a whole roll.

It was during this visit that I discovered the school relied heavily on the Gillingham/Stillman phonetic approach to teach the boys word-attack skills. This method uses cards that have all the different sounds in the English language on them. Each card represents the sound or sounds of a letter or combination of letters. On the front of one card, for example, might be the letter "a." On the back of the card would be:

apple (ă)
baby (ā)
all (â)

On the front of another card might be the letters "oo." On the back of the card would be:

food ($\overline{oo}$)

book ($\breve{oo}$)

Students memorize both sides of the cards so that when they see the letter or letters on the front of the cards they can give the appropriate responses. Thus, a student who saw "a" would respond, "a says (ă) as in apple, a says (ā) as in baby, and a says (â) as in all." Or, a student who saw "oo" would respond, "oo says ($\overline{oo}$) as in food and ($\breve{oo}$) as in book."

Before dinner, Mr. Hayes usually listened to each boy recite the new cards he had learned. Then he and the boy would review some of the cards previously memorized.

I have to admit discovering the Gillingham/Stillman method filled me with mixed emotions. First, I was annoyed that my own well-meaning elementary teachers had made my life so difficult by trying to cram whole words into my head with practically no phonetic instruction. I realized that I could still benefit from the Gillingham/Stillman system as I frequently have difficulty pronouncing words I haven't seen before. Second, it was exciting to discover that, like me, Anna Gillingham had also found the best way to teach a young child was to break a problem into its smallest pieces and teach the child how to use those pieces. But mostly, I felt gratitude and relief that Brian was being taught by people who so obviously knew what they were doing and who had been successful with other learning disabled youngsters.

The teachers at Linden Hill did a lot of their teaching through projects, for they knew that many of the boys learned best when they could actually touch what they were learning. They drew and painted maps on plywood and then cut out the states or countries and played geography games with the finished pieces. Each boy had his own tool kit, and all learned to use the various tools in it. Measuring reinforced mathematical concepts, and using the tools sharpened eye-hand coordination. Even so, the boys had daily writing assignments, and public speaking was encouraged. In fact, there was a yearly competition for the best recital of the Gettysburg Address.

When Brian came home in the middle of February for a holiday, having been at Linden Hill for five months, he announced that he had won the competition for the Gettysburg Address recitation that year.

"Do each of you recite a few lines," I asked, "and the winner is the boy who does his lines best?"

"No, I can say the whole thing. Do you want to hear me recite it?" Brian answered.

"Of course," I said, not really expecting him to get very far.

Brian proceeded to give a spellbinding rendition of the Gettysburg Address. I was floored. Hugging him, I said, "Your performance is outstanding. Even Laurence Olivier couldn't do it better. Let's record it." I ran for my tape recorder, and he recited it again. When he finished, he told me there was an introduction, so I put the recorder back on and we recorded that. Then, his eyes radiant with his success and new self-confidence, he said to me, "I know more," and we recorded his counting to ten in Latin and Greek and reciting a poem about the parts of speech. As I hugged him, I had to fight back the tears. My little boy, whom I'd been told to put in an institution because he would never be able to learn, was performing on a very high level. I knew there was still a long, mountainous road ahead, but I was filled with joy that he had begun the climb.

14

Penny Opens Up

"I'm listening and thinking that I don't want to go to school today."

—Penny

As I began to trace our family's history of learning disabilities in this book, I said to Penny, "It's interesting that your learning disability really didn't become noticeable until you were in the sixth grade."

Penny said patiently, for as the youngest of four she learned patience early in her life, "Mom, I was doing terribly and struggled all the way along. When I began sixth grade, Kelly, Whitney, and Brian were all in boarding schools. It was the first time I was the only one left at home, and you woke up to 'there's Penny.' You realized how little I knew and how poor my academic skills were. Then you began to deal with me."

Her comment made me think back to Penny's second grade at Ridge School. That year, the same tutor who had tutored Kelly while she was at Ridge began to tutor Penny. After the third session, Penny came home in tears, saying, "She calls me Kelly. I don't like being shut in that room with

145

her. I'm not dumb like Kelly, and I don't want to be tutored." I had explained in no uncertain terms that Kelly was not dumb, but then I had looked at her tear-stained face and decided tutoring could wait.

Unlike Kelly and Brian, who were hyperactive, Penny as a youngster was hypoactive. She was reserved, shy, and a dreamer. While staying in touch with reality, she could easily tune out of a difficult situation and allow her creative mind to take her into a happy fantasy land. Penny always knew where she was and what she was supposed to be doing, but she often did not listen. Even I couldn't always tell if she was taking in what I was saying. Sometimes she looked tuned out but could repeat everything I had said. Other times I thought she was absorbing all my words, but I'd realize later that she had heard very little.

One morning, en route to school, Penny seemed to be in another world. I finally said to her, "When you get to school today, I want you to listen and think." When she didn't respond, I asked the inevitable parental question, "Are you listening?" She answered, "I'm listening and thinking that I don't want to go to school today."

Penny preferred to fade into the background. When she was required to talk, she often spoke so softly that it was difficult to hear what she said. Her quiet demeanor, good IQ, and the fact that her learning disability is mild allowed her to get by until the sixth grade.

That year, however, as Penny said, I finally tuned into her academic difficulties. She had been squeaking through for several years now, not so badly that you immediately became worried but not as well as everyone said she could do. It was silly of her, I thought, to bounce from an A to a D in the same class from term to term. I began to tutor her myself and, shortly before final exams, included a friend of hers, who was dyslexic, in our sessions.

Penny's sixth-grade Ridge School final exams were classics. In English, which was the course and teacher she disliked most, students received an enormous list of words with instructions to write an original essay using all the words. Penny's essay was entitled, "I Abhor English," and the last sentence read, "And my English teacher is ostentatious." I gulped when I read the final sentence, and I prayed that Penny's teacher had a sense of humor. Then I asked Penny what *ostentatious* meant. "Well," she replied, "having written that I abhor English, I thought I should end on a positive note. I think it means something nice so I gave her a compliment."

I looked at her in total disbelief. She had been exposed to these words all term. Why didn't she know them? It wasn't as if the vocabulary she heard every day was terribly limited, and there were always dictionaries for her use. I moved on to the next exam.

Her French exam seemed to test her knowledge of geography more than her knowledge of French, but it was revealing. One part of the exam was designed to test a student's knowledge of *de* or *du* before the name of a city or a country. Penny wrote, "Tokyo est la capitale de Paris." She used *de* and *du* correctly throughout the exam but failed because she didn't know cities from countries, much less where they were located.

A part of me wanted to go to her French teacher and say, "But look, she used *de* and *du* correctly. Do the cities and countries really matter? That's not what you're testing." Another part of me said, "Wait. Penny has been learning about cities and countries since second grade. Why isn't she using what she, in theory, knows? Does she really not know the difference between a city and a country?"

On the same exam was the question "What are the colors of the fourth of July?" written in French. Penny thought of the many colors in the fireworks displays on July fourth and wrote in correct French, "All the colors are the colors of the fourth of July." The answer would have been fine, except, at some point, the teacher had given the class a clue that the correct answer was "red, white, and blue." Although the rest of the class had gotten that clue, Penny had missed it. Not paying attention? Perhaps, or perhaps she hadn't been able to pull the clue from the context of the teacher's words. In any event, she got no credit for her answer.

Before her history exam, I had tutored Penny and her friend extensively and felt confident that both girls knew the material well. Not only had they memorized the facts, they even seemed to understand them. Penny's friend, who had a different teacher, did well, but Penny did poorly. Her friend's teacher had used the vocabulary straight from the history book. Penny's teacher had used a different vocabulary from the one in the book. Vocabulary again, I thought. She could understand the material, but change the vocabulary and she was lost.

Later, I simplified the vocabulary used for the questions on Penny's exam for her. "Oh," she said, "Is that what she was asking?" and proceeded to give all the correct answers.

It was time for some more testing. Tests revealed that Penny read quickly when dealing with familiar words but had problems analyzing and breaking down new words. Although her ability to hear was normal, she sometimes "lost" the last half of sentences, which indicated some language processing problems. Sequencing and organizing were difficult for her, so she would become discouraged when she had to explain how she was going to do something. Identifying the main idea of a paragraph, drawing inferences, and generalizing were also difficult for her. She was, like Kelly and Brian, a very concrete thinker. Given time to process information in her own way, she could come up with the same knowledge as the rest of her classmates.

Now that I knew this, I could appreciate the years of work Penny had put in taking in information, processing it in her own way, and then trying to retrieve that information in a way that would match her friends. Those years had left her shy and lacking in confidence. This is typical of learning-disabled children. Lacking confidence, they are hesitant to try new things. They may come to dread tests because they don't know what they are being asked, and they can't finish a test in the time allotted because they read more slowly than others. Thus, they don't have the opportunity to demonstrate what they really know. Fortunately, teenagers today who have been diagnosed as dyslexic can take the College Board's S.A.T. (Scholastic Assessment, formerly Aptitude, Test) untimed or with double the time usually allotted, provided they have been granted extra time on tests during the academic year.

Because Penny's learning disabilities were mild, she had succeeded fairly well in the classroom even though she didn't have all the basic background information she needed. Now, I wanted to be sure she had time to get that information and still feel successful. Since the Ridge School's sixth-grade curriculum ran a year ahead of the public schools, Penny transferred to public school for seventh grade, which gave her a chance to review the material from last year and still succeed in school. With her transfer, Penny began the process of filling in the blanks in her knowledge. It was a long process, but she did it beautifully.

15

Getting to Twenty Years Later

"Hi, Mama—This is Katie. I wish that you could talk to me. I love you. Bye-bye."

—first message my four-year-old granddaughter left on my answering machine

R ecently, when I was cleaning out a bookcase to make room for some new purchases, I came upon Brian's Gettysburg Address tape. It's been over twenty years since we made that tape and almost as many years since I've listened to it. I popped it into my cassette player, and as I listened to it, my tears started to flow. I played it a couple of times, rewound it, and carefully placed it back on the shelf. As I dried my eyes, I thought about the long road each of us has traveled and where we are today.

THE FAMILY

Brian was lucky that he was the third child in our family, and not the only learning-disabled one. All of Brian's problems were more widespread and more severe than Kelly's. Kelly could read easy text in second grade; Brian could read only his name and a few other words at the end of fourth grade. Kelly mastered addition and subtraction with the rest of her class; when Brian's class began long division, he still couldn't subtract one number from another if borrowing was involved. In second grade, Kelly wrote interesting stories in beautiful penmanship; it took Brian six months to learn how to draw the letter X and to place it where he wanted it to go on the page. His penmanship was nearly impossible to read until fifth grade.

Kelly's success was grounded in her sheer determination to succeed. Had I tried to teach Brian the way I initially tried to teach Kelly, he would have felt, as Kelly felt, that I was his enemy rather than his ally. The mistakes I made trying to teach Kelly, I did not make with Brian. Had he been our first child, he might not have succeeded.

Brian was also lucky to have Whitney and Penny, two very giving sisters, on either side of him. For a child, there is no substitute for other children, and Penny was Brian's loyal companion in mischief when she was young. Without the nurturing and companionship of Whitney and Penny, Brian's outcome would certainly have been very different. Through his sisters, Brian learned the rudiments of friendship, of sharing, and of taking turns.

In 1973 Jay and I separated and eventually divorced. I believe that what drove us apart was Jay's inability to communicate and what I saw as his need to put me down. Everyone needs to be nurtured, and while I struggled with the children's problems, I desperately needed to hear that what I was doing was a good effort, even if things seemed not to be working. Like others, I needed to be told that I was loved and appreciated, but that was almost impossible for Jay to do. Eventually, I concluded there was nothing I could do to make him happy, and I was miserable because I had begun to feel bad about myself.

NANCY

Shortly after our divorce became final, I remarried. I remarried even though I had not gotten my heart and my head together. My heart said, "Go for it," while my head said,

"This will be a disaster." My head was right. From my two marriages, I've finally learned that a person who doesn't like himself or herself isn't capable of loving someone else. It took time to get over my hurt and accept the fact that twice I'd married the wrong man.

What emerged in time from the second divorce was a happier, more energized, and more fulfilled me. A me who, for the first time in my life, began to understand myself. With my children grown and no husband to care for, I was free to pursue my own interests. I began to regain my tennis skills, and I helped start a Swedish computerized wheelchair company in the United States.

From 1983 to 1987 I was a research affiliate at MIT in the man/vehicle lab, which is part of the Department of Aeronautics and Astronautics. While there, I was a member of a team looking for a way to separate good readers from dyslexics using eye-movement tests. The research involved computer-generated stimuli that were presented to adult subjects while their eye movements were monitored by infrared sensors and then recorded by computer.

In 1986 I became an associate in neurology at Harvard Medical School and extended my dyslexia eye-movement research to children at Boston's Children's Hospital. We published two papers on this research, one in *Cortex* and one in *Annals of Dyslexia*.

Recently, I have made a new version of Brian's wooden and steel calendar out of 100% blue nylon and clear plastic pockets. The activity cards on this new calendar have a teddy bear instead of a little boy doing all the activities. I call this version "The Show Time Pocket Calendar" and have begun a market research project with mockups in classrooms and homes to evaluate its commercial potential for "normal" five-year-olds as well as for the LD population. Since the Show Time Pocket Calendar is lightweight and inexpensive to make, I'm hopeful I'll find someone to manufacture, market, and distribute it.

While I continue with my dyslexia projects (research, a movie, a video, this book, finding a manufacturer and distributor for the games and calendar) and some other projects and activities, I've entered the grandparent stage of my life. What utter joy to come in, play back my phone messages and hear, "Hi Mama—This is Katie. I wish that you could talk to me. I love you. Bye-bye."

It's too early to know if any of my five granddaughters are dyslexic, but with their family history, we'll be keeping a close watch on them. Fortunately, none have the early problems that Brian had, nor are they hyperactive.

BRIAN

Brian's graduation from high school was a happy day for all of us. His best friend, Debbie, as valedictorian, gave the commencement speech, and Brian won the woodworking award as well as his well-earned diploma.

After four years at Wentworth Institute of Technology, Brian went to work as the assistant director of design at Faneuil Hall in Boston. Although he never got his B.S. from Wentworth, he did earn an associate degree and his private pilot, single engine land license while at college.

Brian's life has continued to be a rollercoaster ride. He opened his own roommate matching business in New York City and a year later, out of money and in debt, had to close its doors. He then tried various jobs, including "Mr. Mom," and eventually, several years ago, became a carpenter foreman in charge of all carpentry for two campuses at a large university.

At thirty-two, Brian is married to a nurse and has two daughters, two and four years old. Since leaving his job recently, he has gutted and remodeled his kitchen and dining room and has returned to school. He is enrolled in a nine-month program to increase his knowledge of cooling systems, electrical engineering, and plumbing. He would like to become the engineering manager of a major facility.

Even now, Brian doesn't enjoy reading. When I asked him to read my book, he accepted a copy of the manuscript, but he said, "You realize, Mom, that if I do read this, it will be the first book I've read since college." He can have all the time he wants, of course.

KELLY

I noted earlier that Kelly's self-image had been badly damaged by the years of frustration and defeat that preceded our understanding of her learning problems. Kelly attended five high schools in four years before she graduated from Wilbraham and Monson Academy in Wilbraham, Massachusetts. It was a very difficult period for both of us. During her sixteenth year, she was in two serious automobile accidents and underwent foot surgery, which resulted in her being temporarily paralyzed and able to walk only with crutches and a brace. For much of this time, she and I were at odds. When things were at their worst, one supposed specialist I had consulted had no answers, but he did remark as I left his office that Kelly would probably not make college. I wondered if she would live to see her seventeenth birthday.

Two years later, at her high school graduation, she was given an award as the most outstanding student in her class. She had started a cheerleading squad from scratch, had been president of the senior class, and had headed the fund-raising drive for the senior class gift to the school. We had finally found the right school and environment for Kelly, and there's a lot to be said just for the process of maturing, too.

Kelly's next four years were spent at Cornell University's School of Hotel Administration in Ithaca, New York. She struggled academically, but she was a shining star in food preparation and presentation, and she successfully organized and directed many major functions. Immediately after the graduation ceremonies, she went to work for a major hotel in Atlanta, where she met and married her husband, who was working for the same hotel. Before a different chain brought her back to Boston, she worked for various hotel companies in Minneapolis, Baltimore, Hilton Head Island, Dallas, and Houston.

For the past fourteen years, Kelly has frequently worked sixteen-plus hours a day, often going weeks without a day off. Her hard work, exceptional talent in her field, mature sense of humor, superb organization, and dedication to detail and follow through, as well as her ability to motivate, develop, and promote her employees, has paid off. Today, Kelly is a corporate food and beverage director for a major hotel chain in the United States, a position so far rarely achieved by women. She is also pregnant with her first child.

PENNY

Brookline public schools began French in the seventh grade, so having had a course in French during her sixth grade at Ridge School, Penny was now able to work a bit less hard on her French as she filled in some of the information gaps in history, geography, and general vocabulary. The public school curriculum moved at a slower pace, which allowed Penny to do better academically with less stress. Still, by the end of her freshman year at Brookline High School, it was evident that Penny needed special help to pick up the concepts and skills she either lacked or had not automatized. She spent her sophomore year of high school at the Hun School in Princeton, New Jersey, where she was involved in their remedial program.

After completing high school and then graduating from the University of New Hampshire, Penny returned to Boston and went to work in a bank's mutual fund department. At the end of her first year, she received an award as the outstanding employee of the bank. Two and a half years later, she was made a supervisor, becoming the youngest administrative officer of the bank, with a salary nearly two and a half times her starting salary. The celebration over this promotion was especially sweet, as a specialist Penny had seen in seventh grade had warned us not to have very high expectations for her.

Today, Penny is married, has a nineteen-month old daughter, and is expecting another baby. She works full time as the assistant comptroller at a large hotel and still wins awards. Last year she received the outstanding manager award at the hotel.

Early in her life, Penny learned to be a good listener, to help others with their problems, and to make people feel good about themselves. Consequently, she has always had lots of friends and, for a long time, has been the peacemaker in our family when one is needed. She has a remarkable gift for being able to tune into the thoughts and moods of those around her and to empathize with them.

WHITNEY

With no learning disabilities at all, Whitney sailed through school. After Ridge School, she attended Andover Academy in Andover, Massachusetts. At graduation she received the Madame Sarah Abbott award, which is given to the most outstanding girl in the senior class as voted by her teachers and classmates. She also received the math award, and she shared the athletic award with another student.

Whitney applied under the early admissions plan to Harvard and was accepted. While she was there, she maintained a high academic average, played in starting positions on varsity teams for four different sports, represented the university in three national athletic competitions, was captain of house crew, played in the band, and was one of four females elected class marshall her senior year.

After graduation, she moved to San Francisco, where she worked in communications. A year after her arrival, she became ill. Although her illness was never diagnosed, she had symptoms similar to those of Epstein-Barr and probably had chronic fatigue syndrome. For years after she first became ill, she was able to work only part time and generally spent more hours sleeping than awake each day.

Whitney has been married now for nine and a half years and has two daughters. For the past five years, she has worked for a software company in the Bay area. Now that she has children, she works three days a week for her company as a consultant and support representative in new product development.

In some ways, Whitney is the rock of our family. Brian has always respected her judgment, and over the years, Penny has often looked to her for information and support, especially since becoming a mother. The friction that seemed to exist frequently between Whitney and Kelly when they were young disappeared as they grew up and came to respect each other's interests and strengths.

Several times a month, Whitney writes to her grandparents, passing on family information, and we all try to gather together at least twice a year. It is important to Whitney that her children get to know their aunts, uncles, cousins, grandparents, and great-grandparents, so these gatherings are wonderful moments of mass confusion, laughter, and discovery.

Some family photographs, including two from recent gatherings, are included at the end of this book. If you skip to the photos, please don't forget to come back and read the Afterword and Representative Resources sections. They provide important information about learning disabilities and the people who may be able to help if *something's not right* with a child or young adult you know.

Afterword

In 1981, the National Joint Committee on Learning Disabilities defined learning disabilities as:

> a heterogeneous group of disorders manifested by significant difficulties in the acquisition and use of listening, speaking, reading, writing, reasoning or mathematical abilities. These disorders are intrinsic to the individual and presumed to be due to central nervous system dysfunction. Even though a learning disability may occur concomitantly with other handicapping conditions (e.g., sensory impairment, mental retardation, social and emotional disturbance) or environmental influences (e.g., cultural differences, insufficient/inappropriate instructions, psychogenic factors), it is not the direct result of these conditions or influences.

Learning disabilities are a root cause of major problems in our society. According to the National Institute of Health, more than 15 percent of students (about one in seven students) in the United States are learning disabled.

It has been estimated that somewhere between 25 and 40 percent of children and adolescents with learning disabilities have apparently inherited them (that is, the characteristic is in their genes). Dyslexia, for example, runs in some families, and that condition or the predisposition for it, given a certain *in utero* environment, is carried by one or more genes. According to the *60 Minutes* documentary "Dyslexia: The Hidden Disability," 10 percent (one out of every ten) of the people in the United States have dyslexia, whereas only 3.5 percent of the population *as a whole* have muscular dystrophy, cerebral palsy, or mental retardation. Although there are studies showing as many girls as boys are dyslexic, most research reflects a higher incidence of boys with the syndrome than girls. For some reason, there are also higher than normal incidences of dyslexia among twins and adopted children.

Today, as more babies with birth weights of three pounds or less are saved, there is an increasing number of children with learning disabilities that are not inherited. In a study published in 1988, researchers at the University of California at Berkeley examined the intellectual and educational status of 108 eight-year-olds who weighed less than 3 pounds 3 ounces at birth. They found 36 percent had no apparent problems. Another 45 percent did poorly on tests of visual-motor coordination, the ability to complete tasks well, and verbal skills, suggesting they were probably suffering from learning disabilities in school. The other 19 percent were mentally retarded.

Although studies have shown a direct correlation between learning disability, lack of academic achievement, school drop out, juvenile delinquency, later crime, and in many cases, incarceration (one New York study showed that 60 to 80 percent of that state's incarcerated population has some form of learning disability), many potentially productive learning-disabled children are neither achieving their potentials nor becoming productive adults. This is occurring even though, over twenty years ago, learning disabilities were recognized by the 94th Congress as one of the handicapping conditions requiring appropriate education under the "Education for All Handicapped Children Act." This act, whose final phase became effective in 1980, was passed to assure free and appropriate education for all handicapped persons ages 3 to 21.

Because specialists do not agree on what constitutes a learning disability and which tests can properly diagnose the condition, it is often difficult, especially when there is a lack of funding, to get school systems to provide the individual attention the child needs or to pay for private school when the public schools cannot meet the child's needs. Even those children who have been tested and provided with an Individual Educational Plan (IEP) are not home free.

Partially because of funding cutbacks in the last several years, many special classes are too large and have youngsters with such diverse skills, learning styles, IQ's, knowledge, and problems that no teacher can adequately deal with each individual's needs. This type of class often leads to a watered-down, sugar-coated curriculum that occupies the child but doesn't do much for the child's education. There are some public and private schools that are doing an excellent job with their learning-disabled population, but most LD youngsters are short-changed educationally, and some are even ridiculed or punished for their mistakes and failures.

The following page has a very brief list of elements that affect the success of working with someone who is learning disabled. Having given this outline, let me add that dealing with the condition is never easy. It takes persistence on the part of the learning disabled and on the part of the people dealing with them. This book can only serve to get you started. If you have a learning-disabled child, this is the first step in a long but very rewarding road. You have a lot of reading and networking ahead of you.

❖　❖　❖

Five months after I finished writing this book, an illness abruptly halted my usual physical activities. Under doctor's strict orders to rest and thus having to spend several hours each day being horizontal, I had the opportunity to think about what I'd written and what I still hadn't said.

Working Successfully with Someone Who Is Learning Disabled

The items listed below are vital in dealing successfully with learning disabilities:

1. **Diagnosis** as early as possible

2. **Understanding,** both by the youngster or adult struggling with the condition and by their caregivers, as to the specifics of how the disabilities are affecting their life

3. **Appropriate remediation** for the specific needs of the individual

4. **Concrete, practical tools,** such as appointment books, prioritized lists of things to do and the times by which they need to be completed, simple filing systems, and so on

5. **An encouraging/reminding person,** that is, a person (a therapist or anyone close to the individual, such as a parent, teacher, tutor, or spouse) who gives structured encouragement and reminders that help the learning-disabled person until they can stay on track themselves

6. **Possibly medication** if the situation is further complicated by factors such as hyperactivity and/or depression, but only trained practitioners can determine this

The missing pieces fell into two categories: (1) information about Attention Deficit Disorder (ADD), which wasn't known when I was raising my family in the 1960s and 1970s, and (2) the saga of what it took to get this story written and published.

ATTENTION DEFICIT DISORDER (ADD)

Since 1980 the term Attention Deficit Disorder (ADD) has become a common label for some children and adults. Sometimes the label is further detailed as Attention Deficit Hyperactivity Disorder (ADHD), when hyperactivity is present, and sometimes as Adult Attention Deficit Disorder (AADD), when the adult stage is the focus of discussion. I want to say a few words about the ADD syndrome, because today if my children were in preschool and early elementary school, three of them probably would be diagnosed ADD with LD.

The symptoms most often associated with ADD are easy distractibility (deficits in consistent attention and effort), impulsivity, the need for frequent and immediate approval, and usually, but not always, excess energy or hyperactivity. Even though there is a higher incidence of ADD in dyslexics than in nondyslexics, ADD and dyslexia are separate syndromes.

ADD is a neurological syndrome whose main cause is genetic. Environmental factors can make it worse, but they do not cause it. It is believed that about one-third of those people with ADD outgrow it. The other two-thirds have it throughout adulthood.

Brian, for sure, was and is ADD/LD. While his incredible hyperactivity disappeared during puberty and he is today extremely well organized, he still struggles with impulsivity, does not always read facial expression, body language and voice intonation appropriately, and often becomes irritated when interrupted. At thirty-two, Brian is good looking, bright, warm, hard-working, and likable but still frequently manages to get himself into very difficult situations.

Kelly continues to be action oriented, always has several projects going simultaneously, and thrives on high stimulus situations and novelty. In recent years, she has learned to handle her mood swings and keep her energies channeled productively. She no longer procrastinates, and she has developed extraordinary organizational skills. While she has successfully learned to compensate for the ADD/LD difficulties with which she was born, she still functions best with immediate validation of what she is doing.

Penny, too, was probably ADD/LD without the hyperactivity element. She was, if anything, underactive and a dreamer. As a youngster she was tuned out much of the time, rarely initiating activities or friendships. Having no idea where to start or how to organize her time and materials, Penny frequently put off doing school assignments and simply escaped into her own fantasy world. Although she was capable, the combination of her learning disability and her habit of tuning out resulted in academic performance that often fluctuated from A to E and back to A in any given course in any given year. Her performances remained inconsistent until her sophomore year in college, when she learned to stay focused until jobs were complete, and her high grades reflected this new capacity. Penny has not stopped day dreaming, but she has learned to stay tuned in when it is necessary.

For those interested in knowing more about ADD, I recommend *Driven to Distraction: Attention Deficit Disorder in Children and Adults* by Edward M. Hallowell, M. D., and John J. Ratey, M. D. Both authors cope with ADD themselves and have practices specializing in the disorder. Their paperback book is published by Pantheon Books in New York.

DETERMINATION WINS OUT

I put off writing this book for a long time, always telling myself I'd better wait a little longer and see how my children turned out. I now suspect I procrastinated because I didn't know how or where to start. I never imagined how difficult writing a book would be or how long it would take.

One day I simply sat down at my computer and began to write. For six months I spent several hours daily in front of the computer. Much of the time I cried—often not knowing what I was crying about. In between bursts of tears, I'd write. At the end of six months, I had written 200 pages. As I gave them to a friend to read, I remarked that I didn't know why it took some people many years to write a book.

Thinking the most difficult part was behind me, I anxiously awaited my friend's review. She began by saying, "Because I'm your friend, I'll give it to you straight. You haven't written a book. This is a mess of interesting but confusing events spread over 200 pages. To begin with, Nancy, books have chapters!"

I then did several rewrites, and from the feedback I got, it seemed the manuscript was not improving. In desperation I hired a writing teacher from Harvard to give me private lessons. I taped all our sessions, and after each class, I'd return home and transcribe the entire lesson. Hearing it several times and writing it provided a way for me to learn what Pamela was trying to teach, but it was an excruciating way for me to learn how to express my own ideas in print. At the end of several months, we both agreed that if my book was ever going to get published, I'd need to have someone co-author or ghost it.

I began the search for a writing partner. It took months to find someone I could afford and whom I was told had good writing skills. Once I had, we spent a year putting together a book proposal. Then I learned one usually needs a literary agent to get a publisher, and my writer did not have an agent and did not know of one I could hire. Although I was told it was hard to find an agent, I finally landed one. My agent worked hard to sell the proposal (the book still wasn't written), but he did not succeed. That ended co-writer number one.

Next, I turned to an old friend who had written two successful movies starring Steve McQueen. Alan coached me on several rewrites, but after a year or so, he too gave up on my book. That ended co-writer number two.

Before I chose another co-writer, I sat down and really thought about what I thought was needed. I decided I wanted a female writer who was a mother who had raised a dyslexic child. Surely she would understand what I was trying to write. I actually found a woman in California who met all the above qualifications, and I hired her. But her draft of what was to be the first chapter didn't match my feelings. I showed it to a writer I had met since the start of my book project and who had become my friend, coach, and confidant. She suggested that I should write a constructive critique of the chapter, which I did. In return, my California writer sent me a nice letter saying she would not be able to write my book to my satisfaction and enclosing the money I had advanced her. That ended co-writer number three.

After many months I hired a young local writer. After we had negotiated an agreement, he began to write. It took him a year to write the book proposal, partially because he writes slowly and partially because his wife had a baby and then took a very demanding job, leaving him to be "Mr. Mom." I liked his sample chapter, but the two literary agents to whom he showed the proposal were not interested in it. One agent suggested that a movie might be the most effective way to tell my story.

My writer then told me of a friend of his who had written an award-winning video. Eventually, the three of us met and worked out an agreement to collaborate on writing a film treatment about raising my children. I also wanted a book, but they wanted nothing further to do with it and insisted that our new contract specify that none of us had any obligation to the other parties regarding the book. That ended co-writers number four and five as far as the book went.

Over the next two years, we wrote several treatments for a movie. Eventually my writers told me my story was too complicated, which, of course, learning disabilities and families often are. I finally agreed to our writing a fictional movie about a young widow struggling to raise her dyslexic son. While working with them on the screenplay, I returned to working on my book.

We finished the script a month before I finished this book. One agency reviewed the screenplay favorably but said it was too soft a property. Then, a television producer from Los Angeles wanted to option the film if we'd do a major rewrite. He actually came to Boston to work on the rewrite, but my attorney was not able to work out an agreement with the two writers. I tabled the movie for the moment and began to look for a book publisher. After two rejections, and in the seventh year of the project, I got lucky.

IN CONCLUSION

I hope my story has provided some insight into the variety of difficulties the learning disabled encounter and how one family coped with them. It's not easy, but with early diagnosis, appropriate education, warmth, understanding and nurturing, the future can be a bright one for the learning disabled.

Margaret Byrd Rawson, speaking at a White House Conference on Handicapped Persons, beautifully stated what I've tried to show in this book. The following is excerpted from her speech. Although it focuses on dyslexia, its applicability to all learning disabilities is apparent.

> Dyslexia is the handicap you can't see, but it is real. It is always hampering and often crippling to the person who has it. Ask that person, sometimes called dyslexic, who has not been able to learn to read, write, and spell his own language in the course of his schooling.
>
> He can tell you how serious the problem is. He feels stupid, and is often thought to be so, although generally he is not.

He may, in fact, be very bright. He seems incompetent and, in this one field, he is, because he has not been able to master the language skills as expected of him in elementary school. . . .

He may get through high school the same way, generally being called lazy, uninterested, or, at best, an underachiever. He may drop out and be unemployed or even unemployable. His way is full of dangers—bad company and undesirable behavior, if not delinquency; discouragement, depression, and unhappiness; dependence, a life on welfare, perhaps prison or a hospital. . . . In spite of his discouragement and frustration, he may "make it" if he gets the right help.

This handicap is very real and has to do particularly with learning language. There are special ways known to teach the language-disabled person, young and old, and they work. With enough of the right kind of help, he can deal with his handicap. It may slow him down but it need not stop him.

But first we must be aware of this hidden handicap, learn more about its nature, see the needs of people who have it, and provide much better than we do now for meeting these needs. These boys and girls and men and women have an access problem as real as that of the wheelchair traveler faced with a steep flight of stairs.

We want to understand the nature of these handicaps and learn how we can all help each of the afflicted persons to meet his difficulties so that the rest of him—generally the largest part of the person—can be free to develop and express his real and potential self.

Representative
Resources

ORGANIZATIONS

For parents who are just beginning to learn about dyslexia or learning disabilities, I recommend the following three organizations as starting points in your voyage to help your youngsters.

1. The Orton Dyslexia Society, for professionals and parents of children and adults with dyslexia, fosters research on the nature of dyslexia and on effective teaching methods and provides information to the press and public. Among its publications are *Annals of Dyslexia*, their interdisciplinary journal, and *Perspectives on Dyslexia*, published four times a year. This nonprofit society has branches in most states in the United States. The national headquarters can direct you to your closest branch.

    The Orton Dyslexia Society, National Headquarters
    Chester Building, Suite 382
    8600 LaSalle Road
    Baltimore, Maryland 21286-2044
    Phone: (410) 296-0232

2. Learning Disabilities Association (LDA) (formerly the Association for Children and Adults with Learning Disabilities), for parents and professionals, is a national parent association with state and local chapters. Its publication is *Newsbriefs,* which is published six times a year. The LDA local groups provide educational programs, advice on local issues and programs, and support systems for parents, families, children, and adolescents. Contact the National Office to locate your nearest chapter.

   LDA, National Office
   4156 Library Road
   Pittsburgh, Pennsylvania 15234
   Phone: (412) 341-1515

3. The Learning Disabilities Network, serving New England and other regions, is a nonprofit organization dedicated to unlocking the potential of those with learning disabilities by providing educational and support services to LD individuals, their families, and the professionals who work on their behalf. Their publication, *Exchange,* promotes communication in the field of learning disabilities.

   The Learning Disabilities Network
   72 Sharp Street, Suite A2
   Hingham, Massachusetts 02043
   Phone: (617) 340-5605

PROJECT ASSIST INSTITUTE

As one example of a successful program for educating LD students within the public school system, take a look at the Project ASSIST Institute (PAI), an Orton-Gillingham/Spalding based curriculum for teachers and volunteers. Project ASSIST

(Alphabetic Sound Symbol Instruction Systematically Taught) Institute is a private, nonprofit corporation dedicated to the advancement of literacy. It provides education for teachers and volunteers in a multisensory, sequential method of intensive phonics. It provides volunteer tutoring teams to public schools, ongoing support to all PAI-educated teachers and volunteers, and speakers for educational and civic groups. PAI strives to expand educational opportunities and services so that its curriculum will be available to all who need it.

> Project ASSIST Institute
> 500 Dunkin Road, Suite A
> Wilmington, Delaware 19809
> *Phone:* (302) 764-1010

BOOKS FOR PARENTS

Today there are many guides for parents that are helpful, but my two all-time favorites, and the ones I highly recommend are these:

> Larry B. Silver, M.D., *The Misunderstood Child: A Guide for Parents of Learning Disabled Children.* New York: McGraw-Hill Book Company, 1984.
> This is a step-by-step guide for helping your learning-disabled youngster. Dr. Silver is dyslexic and, at the time he wrote this book, was Acting Director of the National Institute of Mental Health (NIMH) in Bethesda, Maryland. He discusses the possible causes of learning disabilities, describes the various symptoms, details the social and school problems that can accompany them, and concludes with treatments, the parents' role, and legal issues.

Sally L. Smith, *No Easy Answers: The Learning Disabled Child at Home and at School.* New York: Bantam Books, 1979.

A guide to the basic principles and approaches that help learning-disabled children learn to learn. This book gives anecdotes of dyslexic behavior followed by appropriate ways of dealing with each situation. Sally Smith is the mother of a learning-disabled child, a Professor at the American University, where she is head of their learning disability program, and founder and director of the Lab School for severely learning-disabled children in Washington, D.C.

BOOK FOR PARENTS AND YOUNG ADULTS

This publication has received high marks from many in the field of learning disabilities:

Melvin D. Levine, M.D. *Keeping a Head in School: A Student's Book about Learning Abilities and Learning Disorders.* Cambridge, Massachusetts: Educators Publishing Service, Inc., 1990.

Intended for the nine- to fifteen-year-old, this book gives students with learning disorders an appreciation of their own individuality, a better understanding of their strengths and weaknesses, and specific suggestions for approaching their school work. Cassette recordings of the book are also available from the publisher.

BOOKS FOR YOUNGER CHILDREN

Two books about dyslexia, written for children, are also worthy of mentioning. They are:

Caroline Janover, *Josh: A Boy with Dyslexia.* Burlington, Vermont: Waterfront Books, 1988.

Jeanne Gehret, *Learning Disabilities and The Don't Give Up Kid.* Fairport, New York: Verbal Images Press, 1990.

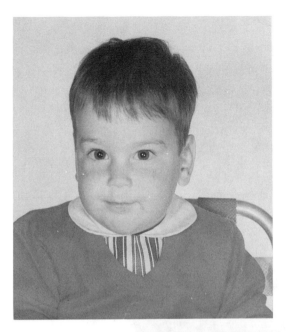

*Brian (16 months)
looking angelic
between outbursts*

*Brian (23 months)
with "Air-we"*

*Penny (5 months), Whitney (4 years 4 months),
Kelly (5 years 8 months), and Brian (23 months)*

*Whitney, Kelly, Brian, and Penny pose during
summer 1964 for upcoming Christmas card;
Kelly about to enter first grade, and Brian at
2 years 3 months*

At 2 years 9 months, Brian showing his frustration, and Brian sleeping half on his bed and half on his night table. These two photos survived my early editing days, when I tried to make Brian "normal" by keeping only happy pictures.

Four-year-old Brian holding Chips, one very nervous dog when in Brian's hands

Brian (4 years old) in one of the cars he loved to ride

Brian (4 years), Penny (3 years), Kelly (8 years), and Whitney (7 years), posing for our 1966 Christmas card

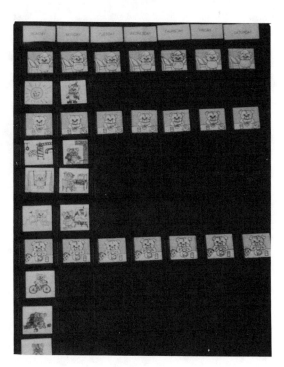

Poolside pose during summer 1967: Penny (about to enter four-year-olds nursery school), Brian (going into kindergarten), Kelly (going into fourth grade), and Whitney (going into third grade)

Portion of a current version of Brian's calendar

In these two pictures, I'm keeping Kelly and Brian company while they are being tested by Dr. Kris at M.I.N.D.

Whitney, Penny, myself, Brian, and Kelly posing with the 1, 2, 3 Instructional Program as it's set up to play (1968)

Cristina Lana visiting for Christmas 1971: Kelly (13 years), Brian (9 years), Penny (8 years), and Whitney (12 years)

Penny-eating Brian-fighting Daddy-tennis Whitney-reading mommy-Hurrying

Help Help

Drawings by Kelly, who was given only a few minutes to render the members of her family during a "kinetic family drawing test" in November 1972, when she was 14 years old. It's amazing to me how succinctly she captured everyone.

Kelly-dancing

Brian (12 years old) with friend David Silver, posing with a complex house of cards they had built

December 5, 1975

Dear Mom,

How are you? I am fine.

I just thought of something I need bad for my go cart. I need 4 wheels. I can get them hear with Tom. They will cost alittl less than 50 dollars. I now that is exspencive, but Tom and I feel those are the ones that we need. The go cart is reely nice, and I cant wait to show you it when it is don.

I all so need some stationarry. I think that I have some att home but Im not sure, allso I need a tie clip to hold my tie out of the soup. Theres allso this reccord that David Silver plays that I woold like to get. I don't now the name of it but David would thow if I asked him. I realy like it and its from the beatuls.

Oh gues what we just started scatting and it was somuch fun. I can't wate to go agan. Are pond is even frozen stif. It has reely gotton colled. It will brobuly snow soon heerto.

The days are going so soon and I cant wate to come home. Do you now if David can come. If he can com please write me and tell me.

Miss you
and Love
you.

A typical letter from Brian while at Linden Hill School; this letter was written while he was in eighth grade, at age 13.

181

Four-generation photo taken in March 1993 of Penny, my parents, Penny's daughter Kristi, and myself

Here I am with my beloved grandchildren during a family gathering in summer 1993. (Photograph by Claire Kaiser)

Index

A Note from the Publisher

If you are a reader who wants to make a proposal to Ms. Lelewer regarding the games or calendar she has described in this book (The 1, 2, 3 Instructional Program or The Show Time Pocket Calendar), please send your proposal or other written material to Ms. Nancy Lelewer, c/o VanderWyk & Burnham, PO Box 2789, Acton MA 01720-6789. We will ensure that she gets your communication. Don't forget to include your return address and telephone number in your letter to Ms. Lelewer so that she can respond.

Do you want more copies of this book?

For complete ordering information, please call toll-free:
(800) 789-7916 *(orders only)*